Math at their own pace

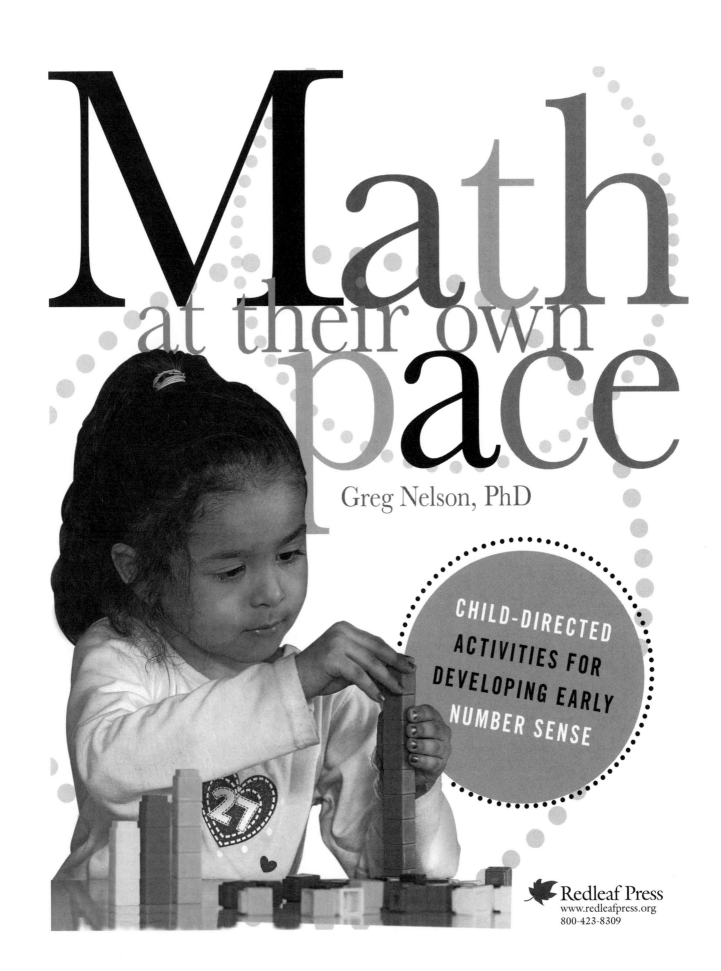

Math at their own pace

Greg Nelson, PhD

CHILD-DIRECTED ACTIVITIES FOR DEVELOPING EARLY NUMBER SENSE

Redleaf Press
www.redleafpress.org
800-423-8309

Published by Redleaf Press
10 Yorkton Court
St. Paul, MN 55117
www.redleafpress.org

First edition 2007

Cover design by Soulo Communications
Cover photograph by Steve Wewerka
Interior typeset in Baskerville and designed by Soulo Communications
Interior photos by the author

Printed in the United States of America
14 13 12 11 10 09 08 07   1 2 3 4 5 6 7 8

Library of Congress Cataloging-in-Publication Data
Nelson, Greg, 1951-
  Math at their own pace : child-directed activities for developing early number sense / Greg
Nelson. -- 1st ed.
     p. cm.
  ISBN 978-1-933653-29-7 (acid-free paper)
  1. Mathematics--Study and teaching (Early childhood)--Activity programs--United States. 2.
Learning by discovery. 3. Number concept in children. I. Title.
  QA16.N47 2007
  649'.68--dc22
                                    2007017000

Printed on acid-free paper

FSC
Mixed Sources
Product group from well-managed
forests and other controlled sources

Cert no. SW-COC-002283
www.fsc.org
© 1996 Forest Stewardship Council

To my parents, Ed and Shirley, my wife, Ann, and my children, Jeff, Steve, and Leah, who on more than one occasion have all had to take it on faith that

- working with children is, in fact, a profession;

- those boxes of rubble in the basement are, in fact, curricula;

- even though no one is paying me to do all that researching, rummaging, purchasing, constructing, and generally disappearing for hours on end to do who-knows-what, it's important that I keep doing it.

Their unflagging support and love through it all have helped me keep the faith. Thank you.

Math
at their own
pace

Acknowledgments xi

Introduction 1

Chapter 1: Getting Started 5

Chapter 2: Awareness of Stable Quantity and Emergence of Counting 15

Quantity-Matching Jars 17

Quantity Sorting 19

Quantity Concentration 21

More-Less-Same Sorting I 23

Dot Plates 25

Mystery Bag Counting 27

Color-Quantity Bingo 29

Stand Up, Sit Down 31

Let's Count Together 33

Hand Game I 34

Tug-of-War 36

Store 38

Showdown 40

Race to 20 42

Graphing Mats and Voting Boxes 44

Counting throughout the Day 47

The Literature Connection 49

Chapter 3: Counting to 10 51

Number Rods 53

Cuisenaire Rods 57

Decimeter Rods 59

Ten Frames 61

Tabletop Rods 64

The Literature Connection 66

Chapter 4: Recognizing and Writing Numerals 0 to 9 69

Sandpaper or Felt Numerals 70

Cornmeal Tray Numeral Tracing 72

Rainbow Numeral Tracing 74

Telephone Dialing 76

Numeral Relay 77

Wikki Stix, Playdough, and Bodies 79

Numeral Sorting 80

Golf 81

Path Card Numerals 82

Classroom Signs 83

The Literature Connection 84

Chapter 5: Connecting Numerals to Quantities 85

Pencil Boxes 86

Unifix Stairs 89

Numeral Tiles for Tabletop Rods 91

Plates and Clothespins 93

Picture-Sorting Sets 95

More-Less-Same Sorting II 96

Number-Numeral Concentration 98

Number-Numeral Bingo 100

Number-Numeral Mystery Bag I 102

Number-Numeral Mystery Bag II 103

Feed the Squirrel 104

Ten Frame Twister 105

Number Art 107

The Literature Connection 109

Chapter 6: Emergence of Part-Whole Awareness 111

Hand Game II 113

Cover Up 116

Bears in a Cave 118

Shaker Boxes 120

Toothpick Designs 122

Domino Sorting 124

Workjobs Mats 127

How Many All Together? 129

Disappearing Act 131

Handfuls Game I 133

Parts-of Puzzle Cards 134

Flip Book 137

Closer To 140

I Wish I Had 142

How Many Ways Can You Make It? 144

Egg Carton Sum Shaker 146

Balance-Scale Problems 148

Pattern Block Addition 150

The Literature Connection 152

Chapter 7: Counting Higher 153

Piggy Bank 155

Toothpick Shaker Estimation 157

Handfuls Game II 159

What's Missing? Number Charts 160

The Literature Connection 162

Chapter 8: Miscellaneous Games 163

Board Games 164

Quantity Match or Quantity-Numeral Match 165

One More or One Less 165

Racetrack 165

Worm Hunt 166

Card Games 167

Pick a Pair 167

We're Number One 167

Five in a Row 167

Going on a Pair Hunt 168

Blast Off 168

Crazy Eights 168

Snap Variations 169

Games from Around the World 170

Mancala (African and Asian) 170

Dreidel (Hebrew) 171

Toma-Todo (Mexican) 171

Patolli (Aztec) 172

Lu-Lu (Hawaiian) 172

Kawasusuts (Native American; tribe unknown) 173

Miscellaneous Activity Formats 174

Beanbag or Ringtoss Variations 174

Hopscotch Twister 174

Blizzard 174

Commercial Games 176

Hi Ho! Cherry-O 176

Chutes and Ladders 176

Number Neighbors 176

STEP 1–25 Board 177

Mathematics Pentathlon, Division I 177

Appendix: Reproducibles 179

acknowledgments

Like most people who have been in this business as long as I have, I find it impossible to sort out when I first came up with certain activities and with whose help, and which activities are in fact my own creations. The truth is, there are very few new things under the sun. It is the sum that is uniquely my own, not necessarily the parts.

That said, several people I know have had a significant influence on my work, and they deserve mention here. My mentor in my early Montessori years was Dr. Peggy Loeffler. I remember her presentation at a Montessori training at which she dumped a sawed-up set of number rods on the table. There was an audible gasp when people saw what she had done to a sacred—and expensive—piece of Montessori equipment, but I was fascinated. Her innovative approaches to helping children explore their logical and mathematical reasoning helped me escape the confines of prescribed curricula and start looking at learning from the children's point of view. Her passion and insights continue to inspire me today. In my early years of experimenting with modifications of the math curriculum, Margaret Biggs was a creative and perceptive co-conspirator. I had many exciting exchanges with her in which we compared what we were trying in our classrooms and what the children were showing us. More recently, I have enjoyed many thought-provoking conversations with Rebecca Corwin, a fellow faculty member at Bridgewater State College and a former math curriculum developer at TERC.

A number of educators whom I have seen on the national stage but met only in passing have greatly expanded my vision. I remember when John Van de Walle published his textbook on math education. I thought, "Now I don't have to write my book. He's already written it for me." Since then, Juanita Copley has done some remarkable work in expanding our vision of what early childhood mathematics should look like. And Susan Schifter, Susan Jo Russell, and their colleagues in Connecticut have published some marvelous vignettes of child-centered math in classrooms that help all of us see what is possible and how to do it.

I also must thank my editor, Amanda Hane. Through her patient encouragement and carefully considered suggestions, each draft of this manuscript has become clearer and more user-friendly than the last. Finally, I want to thank Bridgewater State College for allowing me to use my sabbatical to work on this manuscript. Without the gift of time, my good intentions of taking this work to the next level would undoubtedly still remain at the "I should" stage.

As important as it is to give other people credit, it is equally important for this son of Missouri to state "The buck stops here." I take full responsibility for any errors of fact and any pedagogical flaws that you find here. Some of these activities occurred to me while I was writing and have not been properly field tested. I hope to spend more time in the next few years systematically researching their impact on children's learning.

I heard it said once that Piaget's greatest contribution was that he gave a whole generation of researchers and educators a new place to stand so they could take his work apart and reassemble it in new and interesting ways. I got where I am through the wisdom and hard work of others, for which I am very grateful. This book is my way of paying it forward.

introduction

Sadly, most of what we think we know about math is mistaken. We may think that math is hard. We may think that it is about right and wrong answers. We may have learned that there is only one way to solve math problems and that we need to have someone teach us what that way is. We may think that math is about memorized facts and that the only way to get good at it is by repetitious drill. And perhaps worst of all, we may think that math is dreadfully, dreadfully boring. Fortunately for us, none of these statements is true.

So how did we come to be so mistaken about math? Probably because most of us were taught math this way—through endless drills, with an emphasis on solving problems a particular way and coming up with the right answers. This means that most of us were, in fact, taught very little math at all. Math is about thinking and problem solving. What we were taught instead was arithmetic. Arithmetic is about computing answers, usually by plugging numbers into fixed rules and formulae. When the emphasis is on teaching arithmetic, there is little time to talk about where mathematical procedures come from or why they work or how other people in other times did math differently. The tragedy of all this is that it is arithmetic that confuses young children, not math. Children are natural mathematicians, but when we prematurely emphasize arithmetic, we cut them off from developing—and trusting—their mathematical minds.

It is no wonder that we tend to teach math in developmentally inappropriate ways, through the same sort of drills and rote memorization we were taught. It is also understandable that most of us in early childhood education have concluded we should spare the little ones from being burdened by math as long as possible. For now, we say, let them be children. The sad truth is that few young children in this country spend time in settings that regularly and deliberately encourage them to engage in deep mathematical thinking. The number of people who are skilled at creating these experiences for children is rather small, and it doesn't include the vast majority of people who actually work with young children on a day-to-day basis.

However, it's not the fault of the frontline troops that too little high-quality math is done in early childhood settings. The fault lies instead with those of us who know how to provide these experiences. We teach our college courses, and we lead our professional development workshops and in-services, and then we leave, knowing full well that without further modeling, encouragement, and material support, most of our advice won't make it into the classrooms of the practitioners we just taught. If we want to do a better job of getting our ideas into widespread use, we need to put into teachers' hands some practical tools that can help them create powerful, stimulating math environments without becoming math experts themselves.

This book is my attempt to provide those resources—to move a step beyond the you-should to the here's-how-to stage. Between these covers you will find a large number of high-quality starting points for hands-on, developmentally appropriate mathematical inquiry. I believe that these activities can help you get started on the right path. Once on that path, I think you'll stay on it, because you and the children will realize together that mathematical learning can be deep and strong, without coercion and pain. You'll also discover what you knew all along but forgot somewhere on the way: we are by nature mathematicians, and doing math is fun.

The Goals of This Book

If this book accomplishes its purpose, I hope we will see more math that is more appropriate and individualized being done more often and by younger children. It's worthwhile to spend a moment clarifying what I mean by each of these objectives and why I think each is important.

More Math

Traditionally, we don't include enough math materials in the environments we set up for young children, nor do we engage in enough mathematical interactions and conversations with children. This book will help you incorporate more math materials into your classroom so that children will have plenty of opportunities to explore mathematical concepts.

More Appropriate Math

Most of the math that we do introduce to young children focuses either on rote counting or on learning the numerals 1 to 10, activities that don't fully challenge them. Some providers move to the opposite extreme and start drilling children on arithmetic algorithms (that is, the specific steps needed to figure out a math problem). Both of these efforts are misguided. In the early years we should provide children with a broad range of experiences and activities to help them develop their logical-mathematical minds through flexible mathematical problem solving. The activities in this book are all open-ended and hands-on. They include variations for exploring concepts in many different ways. Math is more than mere counting, and it has little to do with memorizing steps.

More Individualized Math

Many of the math activities children experience in early childhood settings are teacher-led or done as a group and don't take into account the wide range of abilities and interests among individual children. Most of the activities in this book are of a different sort: they are child-directed, meaning that children can choose when and how they want to engage with them. When children self-select activities at opportune times individually, in pairs, or in small groups, the task can fit their current needs and interests. This maximizes their learning.

Math More Often

Math tends to be a minor presence in most early childhood settings, and the math activities that are present tend not to rate very high on the excitement meter. As a result, not much math gets done. In fact, most of the high-quality math young children do in early childhood settings occurs spontaneously during otherwise non-mathematical events, such as dramatic play or block play. Such moments are important, but they are not sufficient. In this book, you'll find any number of ideas for building math into your classroom so that math games and activities become a staple of your learning environments.

Math at a Younger Age

We tend to hold off on doing much challenging math with young children in order to save them from premature academic study (often termed *push-down curriculum*). Young children are ready now for the math I outline here; they can begin exploring the early activities at as young as two years of age.

Imagine Math in Your Classroom

If we change our understanding about what math is and how children become good at it, a whole new world emerges in our classrooms. Wouldn't it be nice if

- you could stop worrying about forcing children to learn math because you see your children enthusiastically choosing the math activities you add to their environment—and asking for more?

- you could stop resisting standards because you send the children in your program into the early grades as already enthusiastic and productive mathematicians?

- you had the tools to help young children who are already falling behind their peers and who view themselves as mathematical failures—and those tools did not rely upon dull, repetitive drills?

This book is an important resource in getting you and your children there. I encourage you to experience the mathematical sophistication, intelligence, and enthusiasm that young children demonstrate when you provide them with mathematical materials and experiences that are developmentally appropriate yet still challenging. These experiences don't need to be forced upon children. They're hungry for them. So let's begin.

getting started

Many activity books and out-of-the-box curricula hand teachers prefabricated games and activities with instructions for playing or doing them with the children. That's not what happens with this curriculum. Effort *is* required on your part up-front. You'll need to acquire and assemble the materials for these activities and figure out how to make physical space for this curriculum in your environment. But once the children are engaged in the activities, you'll get to spend the majority of your time observing the children and contemplating how to best influence their mathematical play rather than directly teaching them. Preparing the environment so that children can mostly teach themselves is well worth the effort.

The activities in this book work best if the children select them themselves—what they want to do, when, for how long, and how often. Therefore, I encourage you to implement my suggestions as a *shelf-based curriculum*, with a wide assortment of activities preassembled and routinely available on shelves for children to take out as part of their choice time. Why? Interest is a prime ingredient in purposeful activity and thinking, and children get maximal benefit from activities when

1. they are developmentally ready

2. they are intrinsically motivated

3. they can do the activities on multiple occasions

Activities that are out on the shelf as part of a well-stocked center that children have frequent access to meet these three criteria.

What Preparations Do I Need to Make?

For this curriculum, you'll need to create space in your classroom and gather and construct some basic materials before the children can explore the activities.

The Space

To get the maximal benefit from this curriculum, you'll need to devote a lot more of your valuable floor, shelf, and storage space to math activities than you are accustomed to. You might create a math area with the activities arranged attractively in plastic storage boxes on a shelf. Include a table in the area for the children to work at, or stake out some floor space that's free of traffic and comfortable for the children to sit and play on.

The Materials

Since this is a hands-on curriculum, you'll need to spend some time gathering, purchasing, and constructing materials for the activities. Keep in mind that this is a long-term investment— you're not just developing activities for a day or for a week. You're developing curriculum materials that you can use day after day, week after week, and year after year. Take the time to make them well from durable materials. Try to make them as neatly as possible too—your pride in the assembly and display of the materials makes them more appealing to the children and communicates that these materials have value.

Although labor-intensive up-front, this curriculum needn't be expensive. I'm a notorious scrounger, and I would much rather put together a functional activity from scrap and recycled materials than use a fancy store-bought model. Homemade communicates something to the children: it says that math doesn't have to come from the store—that they can explore math with the materials commonly found around them.

Most of the materials can be made with tools no more sophisticated than scissors or a good box cutter, some tagboard (tagboard is the stiff paper material that picture mats are made of—you can often solicit donations of scrap material from a framing shop), and a set of permanent markers. You'll also find templates for some of the materials in the appendix, which you can photocopy, cut out, and glue to sturdy cardboard or tagboard so that they are easy for little fingers to manipulate. Whenever possible, make your own materials or add your own touches to the templates.

Some of the homemade materials require a bit more work, especially those made from wood. These projects are identified by this icon:

CONSTRUCTION
REQUIRED

If you're uncomfortable working with wood, try soliciting volunteers, such as parents in your program or neighbors, to make the materials. If you give detailed specifications to someone who knows how to use a table saw, it doesn't take long to cut the pieces needed from scrap wood. However, if you're still at a loss for woodworkers, I provide suggestions for alternative materials that accomplish the same task and are easier to make. I would much rather have you use whatever you can manage than have you skip the activity altogether because you felt the materials were too hard to construct.

I frequently refer to some standard math materials in these activities, such as Unifix cubes (small colored plastic cubes that link together) and Cuisenaire rods (small wooden or plastic rods in color-coded lengths). These can be found in many educational supply stores and catalogs. You might start with Lakeshore Learning Materials (www.lakeshorelearning.com), Didax (www.didax.com), EAI Education (www.eaieducation.com), or Discount School Supply (www.discountschoolsupply .com) to see what these materials look like and how much they cost.

A handful of the activities use materials that are variations of common Montessori equipment. Montessori materials are very well made but also very expensive, so I usually construct my own. You'll find detailed instructions for making your own sets, but if you want to look at the real thing and see what it costs, I suggest using the list of suppliers on the Montessori Foundation's Web site (www .montessori.org, then navigate to Suppliers—Montessori Materials). Activities that use commercial or Montessori equipment are identified by this icon:

COMMERCIAL
PRODUCT

A NOTE ON MEASUREMENTS

I have intentionally scaled everything in this book to the metric system, referring to centimeters, decimeters, and meters rather than to inches and feet—measurements with which you are probably more comfortable. I have an agenda here. We adults need to make the switch to the metric system, and we definitely need to raise the next generation to be comfortable with the measurement system that's the standard for the rest of the planet. Don't let unfamiliarity with measurement terms such as *decimeter* turn you off to the activities themselves.

How Many of the Activities Should I Set Out at a Time?

Once you have created the materials for these activities, you'll need to set some of them out for the children to use. But which ones do you set out? Certainly the choices offered in this book could overwhelm any child (much less any teacher). They needn't all be available all the time. In fact, periodically changing what's on the shelves helps rekindle the children's interest in the math area.

When deciding which activities to put on the shelf, you should choose activities representing a wide range of skill levels. Children naturally gravitate toward the ones that are the right fit for them. This means you'll probably have a small number of activities from several chapters of this book out on your shelves at any given time. You can certainly pull out other activities when children ask for them specifically or when you think that one would be a perfect next step for particular children. This book is designed to give you a vast pool of options to choose from; use it to make the day-to-day and moment-to-moment decisions that will keep your math curriculum alive, relevant, and interesting.

How Can I Make Sure the Children Actually Do the Activities I Set Out?

What would seem to be the obvious solution—to schedule periods during which children do particular mathematical activities—doesn't work well in practice. As I've already said, what makes the design of high-quality early childhood environments tricky—and what endlessly frustrates legislators and other laypeople—is that children learn best when they choose what and when to do something. Therefore, the way we get children to choose the activities we think are important is to make the activities so attractive to children that they happily select them.

But be careful what you consider attractive. We live in an age in which we often settle for superficial attractiveness in our offerings to children. We make things pretty, or we make them cute, or we make them electronic. The attractiveness to which I refer is of a deeper sort. It is the task itself that should be inherently interesting and fulfilling. In the case of math, that's not hard to do. Children love mathematical problem solving. They are eager to exercise and demonstrate their mathematical intelligence. If we give them an environment in which they can constantly find experiences that feed and nourish their naturally mathematical minds, they'll take it from there.

When you lay out the activities in an attractive manner and at a variety of skill levels, the children won't just settle for the easiest activities. In fact, they most enjoy activities that make them think a little. Their greatest joy comes from struggling for a while and then finally succeeding—there's nothing that beats that feeling of "Yes. I did it." You can create an environment that is joyful *and* rich in mathematical learning—you don't have to choose one or the other.

What Is the Age Range for These Activities?

Two-year-olds can benefit from the beginning activities, which do not require the ability to count. Many first graders would also benefit from spending more time on these activities and less time on the activities they typically encounter in their classrooms. I even know some struggling second, third, and fourth graders who need to spend more time with some of these activities so they can start making sense of the math they are failing to master.

Note that I do not provide suggested age ranges for individual activities. This is because different children develop skills at different points. Match activities not by age but by what the child currently knows and is interested in.

So how can you tell what skill level an individual child should be working at? The chapters that make up this book parallel what we know about how children's mathematical skills develop. The activities in each chapter create the foundational skills needed so that children will be ready for the activities in subsequent chapters. So, for example, children who are just beginning to develop their number sense will be working mostly with activities found in the early chapters. Children who are becoming more competent with numbers will gravitate toward activities found in the later chapters.

At the beginning of each chapter, you'll see a checklist of ways to tell if the children you're working with are ready for the activities in the chapter. For example, if they have mastered counting objects up to 10 but still struggle to name low numerals when shown them, you may pull out some activities from chapter 4. Each activity has a Concepts and Skills Being Learned section to help you pinpoint whether it is suitable for a particular child.

The activities can also be tweaked to match an individual child's skill level as well as to make it possible for children at different skill levels to play together. Each activity has a basic design that targets certain abilities, but it also comes with a host of extensions and variations to bring skill levels up, to bring skill levels down, or to use the same skills in different ways. You can use your own skills as an observer and teacher to adjust activities so that children can be challenged as well as successful. In fancy educational lingo, this is known as *scaffolding* or *keeping children in their zone of proximal development*.

Let me caution you here about rushing children on to the next step. Don't make the mistake of believing that as soon as children show evidence of a particular ability, they should move on to something harder. We tend to be too quick to check off a particular skill or idea once we see evidence of it. For a skill or concept to lodge firmly in place, it needs to be practiced in a wide variety of contexts and over an extended period of time. Many activities in this book offer children opportunities to practice identical skills with different materials or with slightly different procedures. For young children, if an activity *looks* different, it *is* different. Boredom, not familiarity, indicates that children are working below their appropriate level.

What Role Does the Teacher Play?

Most of the activities in this book are ones that children can do on their own, with no teacher present. The goal is for them to be able to choose the materials and proceed with the activities without your help. This does not mean, however, that they will know what to do with the materials when they first encounter them or that they'll always use them appropriately.

When you add these materials to the classroom, ensure that they don't simply become props for the children to use for open-ended play. The number rods are not intended to be horsies for riding or brooms for sweeping. The math materials have a purpose, and part of the children's decision to use them is agreeing to use them for their intended purposes.

This means that the children need to be introduced to the materials. This can be done as part of group time or individually with children who show an interest and readiness. The introduction might involve partnering with a child to model the activity or supervising two or more children as they go through the steps for the first time. Most often, an introduction teaches children how to do the basic activity described in each lesson. The extensions and variations generally come later, once the basic activity is understood. Variations bring the difficulty level up or down, allow different skills to be practiced, or rekindle interest.

Once you have introduced the activities to the children, you may also need to remind them how to use the materials respectfully, as tools for exploring mathematical ideas. Approach children who are abusing materials and say, "I'm sorry. If you're not going to take care of our classroom materials, you should not be using them. Please put them away for now." If children are using pieces of activities as part of non-mathematical pretend play, you can say, "Those are our math materials. If you don't want to do a math activity with them, you should put them away." To give children the freedom to educate themselves with these materials, place some limits on how they use them.

Even though children are essentially teaching themselves and each other through these activities, you still have a vital role to play in turning their experiences into broad and rich understandings. For example, you can

- use what you know about children to influence their choices

- help children use the materials to better fit their individual abilities or to re-spark their interest

- provide additional materials that help children be more successful or explore mathematical concepts in a different way

- provide hints that help children think about the problem in new ways so they can experience greater success and greater learning. For example, you might say,

  - "Would it help to line them up side by side?"

  - "Maybe if we got some counters, we could figure this out."

  - "Would counting them help?"

  - "Here's a number line. See if that helps you."

- partner with children in their activity; this gives you the opportunity, when it's your turn, to talk out loud about what you are doing or use a strategy that the children haven't thought of, or intentionally make an error and let the children catch you at it

- have conversations with the children, especially in the form of open-ended questions that encourage them to think about what they are doing and why they are doing it that way. For example, you could say,

    - "I don't understand what you just did. Can you explain it to me?"

    - "Is there any other way you could do that?"

    - "You said they are both 4, but they don't match. I wonder why that is?"

    - "How can this one be a bigger number than that one? That one is more full."

    - "Is 9 more than 7? How can we find out for sure?"

- join in their excitement and celebrate their accomplishments; help them realize how smart they are and what they have just accomplished. As far as they know, they've just been playing. However, be careful not to simply praise the children with empty phrases such as

    - "Good job."

    - "Nice work."

    - "I like that."

- instead, encourage them by using more meaningful phrases that focus on the child, the specific task they have just accomplished, or the strategy they have used, such as

    - "I like the way you organized the materials. That made counting them a lot easier."

    - "I've never seen it done that way. That's amazing. Do you mind if I take a picture of it?"

    - "How you figured that out is interesting. Tell me about it."

    - "That was a hard problem, but you figured it out. You must be pretty proud of yourself."

    - "You're so smart. Can you explain to Alexa how you did that?"

    - "Look at that. You both did it a different way, and you both came up with the answer."

- document the work that's being done in your class to spotlight interesting discoveries or remind the children of their learning. For example, you might

    - take pictures of some of the things the children have done and have the children dictate what they were doing in the photos

    - have them share their mathematical discoveries with their peers at circle time

- include evidence of the children's mathematical work in their portfolios, their progress reports for their parents, or your newsletter. Remember, because these activities are primarily hands-on, no one will know about them unless you tell them.

A NOTE ON COMPETITION

Many of us in the early childhood field have been taught to discourage competition in our classrooms in favor of cooperative activities. You'll find that the majority of the activities in this book are cooperative. For example, one child provides the prompt for another child to respond to, after which they switch roles. However, some activities involve taking turns or working independently toward the game's objective—and such activities can look a lot like competition. I have included such activities for a reason.

I don't try to eliminate competition from children's lives. I treat it the same way I treat other touchy subjects, such as swearing and refusing to share. I would much rather have these happen in my presence—when I can influence how children respond to them—than ban them entirely from my classroom. At its best, competition can be a way to better ourselves through shared experience. Children engage in more interesting mathematical thinking when they do these activities with other children instead of alone, and competitive games are one way to stimulate shared experiences.

If you look more closely at these activities, you'll see that the emphasis is not on winning. Children quickly shift into playing again instead of dwelling on who won and who lost. The fact that someone got there first—that is, won—basically signals that the round is over and a new round can begin. It's fairly easy to monitor the children's interactions—and talk with them if necessary—to make sure "winners" are being gracious and "losers" are not getting discouraged.

Terms

Finally, there are some mathematical terms I use routinely in this book that may need clarification:

Number: A counted quantity of objects (for example, three blocks). We teach children about numbers by letting them explore quantities in the physical world, which is where children are most comfortable.

Quantity: An amount of objects. Children begin to develop a sense of quantity (for example, *more, less, a lot*) long before they learn how to count, and it takes a while for *quantity* and *number* to mean the same thing to them.

Numeral: A written symbol representing a certain quantity (for example, 3). Numerals are more abstract than numbers. Young children know what to do if we show them 3 blocks, add 4 more blocks, and then ask them how many blocks there are all together. They are at a loss, however, if we show them $3 + 4 =$ and ask them to provide the answer.

Manipulatives: Any objects used by children for their explorations of quantity. Children often use manipulatives to count, sort, or represent a quantity concretely (for example, they use 6 stones to represent the 6 children in a story who each want their fair share of crackers).

Counters: A set of objects provided specifically for counting. These might be commercial objects, such as Unifix cubes, or everyday objects, such as lima beans. If you are working with very young children, be sure to choose manipulatives and counters that are large enough not to pose a choking hazard.

Numeral cards: Rectangular cards made out of tagboard showing numerals.

Picture cards: Rectangular cards made out of tagboard showing a quantity of icons, such as circles, butterflies, or blocks.

Key cards: Often an activity calls for children to sort objects by category (for example, red) or by quantity (for example, 9). Key cards are labels for the category and are set out before children start sorting materials. Key cards for quantities can either be numeral cards, picture cards, or cards showing both a numeral and a pictured quantity. When key cards display a category such as "red," picture icons can be used to label the sets instead of or in addition to words or numerals, since many children are at the prereading stage.

Final Thoughts

There's nothing revolutionary about this curriculum. As early childhood educators, we know that our rooms work best when children choose their own activities. That's why we usually set them up with open-ended interest areas for children to visit again and again. We know that their interest is key and that one-shot experiences usually have little lasting effect. We also know that the teacher's role is to set the stage and the boundaries of acceptable usage, to observe carefully, and to be a respectful partner with children as they explore and invent.

We have tended to forget these principles when it comes to math, however, or the materials we place in the math area are so dreadfully uninteresting that they seldom get used. But once you begin using the activities I describe here in your classroom, you'll find that you already know how to implement this curriculum. Children will flourish as young mathematicians exploring a mathematically rich laboratory. Enjoy.

2

awareness of stable quantity and emergence of counting

Children do not have in-born skills for counting quantities. Their early awareness of quantity comes from visual inspection and intuitive feelings for a few or a lot. This intuitive sense can be fooled by the size of objects or the way that objects are arranged. For example, if you move objects around, young children sometimes think that their quantity has changed. Even if they have counted the objects before and after you moved them, even if they agree that the number has not changed, they nonetheless believe that the quantity has changed. According to constructivist theorist Jean Piaget, these children lack conservation and are at the pre-operational stage of development.

At this stage, young children need lots of opportunities to explore and compare quantity without being prompted to count. As teachers, we should have lots of conversations about relative quantity without making reference to numbers. For example, you might ask,

- "Which do you think has more?"

- "Can you show me why that one has less?"

- "You think I have more, but I think we have the same. How can we find out?"

Through lots of hands-on experiences identifying and comparing quantities, and lots of conversations about how many there are and whether the amount has changed, children gradually come to distrust their visual impressions, discovering instead that quantities can be counted and, once counted, known.

At this early stage, we also want to support children's experiences with counting. In order to develop the mechanics of accurate counting and to discover the relationship between counting and quantity, children need to know

- the number names to say

- the order in which to say the number names

- when counting a quantity, they must say a new number name each time they point to a new object (one-to-one correspondence)

- each object must be counted once and only once

- the last number name said in the counting sequence tells how many objects there are (the *cardinality* principle)

Children initially lack these skills or, if they've acquired them, often fail to use them, because they don't realize their importance. Their first attempts involve frequent errors, but eventually the skills become habitual.

Children's counting errors should not be challenged directly. Instead, we should continue to model counting procedures through our own actions. For example, we might say, "I wonder how many there are? Let me see—one . . . two . . . three . . ." pointing slowly and deliberately at the objects as we count. Be careful to wait patiently while children practice counting for themselves rather than counting for them. In early childhood classrooms, children often count together as a group, such as during circle activities, but in these settings those children who are shaky counters tend to shadow what others around them are saying rather than working on their own counting skills. At this stage, children need lots of experiences with individualized, hands-on counting, like the activities provided in this chapter.

When a stable sense of quantity and the basics of counting come together, children are ready to proceed. These two skills start to come together when children work with small quantities, usually those of no more than 5 or 6. Humans have a visual quantity recognition system called *subitizing* that allows us to recognize a small quantity of objects (for example, 4 spoons) as constituting the quantity 4 without having to count them individually. When we keep quantities small, children are better able to see that quantities are the same, even when they look different. They are also able to count more accurately when they don't have to count beyond 5 or 6. In this chapter, you'll find lots of activities that help children compare and count small quantities.

You know children should be working with the activities in this chapter if

- they show little skill at counting (using wrong number names or names in the wrong order, not counting in a one-to-one fashion, not paying attention to which objects they have counted and which ones they have not, not knowing when to stop counting, etc.)

- they have little sense of how many objects they have, even after having counted a set

- they simply count again when asked how many are in a set they have just counted

- they are uncomfortable with number questions for quantities greater than 4 or 5

- they make their judgments of how many based on visual impressions

Quantity-Matching Jars

Materials and Setup

☐ Ten clear, identical, unbreakable jars with lids

☐ Assorted small objects of different sizes and types in quantities of 1 to 5. Examples include cotton balls, buttons, marbles, balls of aluminum foil, paper clips, toy race cars, beans, grains of rice

Place 1 to 5 objects in each jar so that you have 2 jars for each quantity. Objects within each jar should be the same, but each jar should contain a different set of objects, including the jars with matching quantities. For example, the pair of jars with 2 objects might contain 2 buttons in one jar and 2 cotton balls in the other.

Basic Activity

1 Children find the jars that contain the same quantity of objects and put those 2 jars together.

2 They then arrange the sets in order from least to greatest, 1 to 5.

Extensions and Variations

- Include two empty jars to introduce the concept of zero or none.

- Children work in pairs, alternating who picks the first jar and who finds its match.

- Hold up a jar and ask, "Can you find a jar that has fewer (or more) objects in it than this one?"

- Change the objects in the jars frequently. Consider using seasonal objects.

- For children who can count and know their numerals 1 through 5, provide numeral cards for them to place in front of the appropriate pairs. (See page 13 for more information on numeral cards.)

Concepts and Skills Being Learned

- Quantities can be the same even when the objects themselves are different. Young children don't initially separate the quantity of objects from the objects themselves. For them, 6 beans and 6 toy race cars have nothing in common. This activity helps them to see that quantity is a way of sorting objects.

- Quantities can be different even when the objects are the same (for example, a jar containing 2 crayons does not match a jar containing 5 crayons).

- The size of objects does not affect the quantity of objects. Even though the jar with 2 cotton balls is more full than the jar with 4 buttons, it contains fewer objects. This is a new way of looking at the terms *more* and *fewer* from the child's point of view—one that takes some getting used to.

- Solving quantity problems by visual means. Even young toddlers have the ability to recognize the difference between small quantities by sight. For example, they can see that 4 balls are more than 3 balls, even though they cannot yet count. Again, this is known as *subitizing*.

ADVICE COLUMN

Initially, children view counting and knowing how-much as separate and distinct skills. At this early stage, if something looks like more, it *is* more. Don't prompt children to count objects. Instead, observe whether they choose to count on their own. This is a better marker of whether or not they already consider counting a useful strategy for figuring out quantity.

To help children make these discoveries, use words such as *more*, *less*, and *the same* instead of specific numbers. You might ask,

- "Are these the same amount?"

- "Does this one have more?"

- "Which one has less?"

These are preferable to "How many is that?" or "Can you find the one that has 3?" Only refer to numbers if children have already introduced them into the conversation.

Quantity Sorting

Materials and Setup

- [ ] 20 to 25 clear, identical, unbreakable jars with lids

- [ ] Assorted small objects of different sizes and types in quantities of 1 to 5. Examples include cotton balls, buttons, marbles, balls of aluminum foil, paper clips, toy race cars, beans, grains of rice

- [ ] Key cards for numbers 1 to 5. (See page 13 for more information on key cards.) Younger children figure out the quantity pictured on the cards. Older children read the numerals

Basic Activity

1 Place the objects in the jars in quantities of 1 to 5. You should create 4 or 5 jars for each quantity. The items within each container should be identical.

2 Children lay out the key cards in order from 1 to 5.

3 They examine the objects in each container and place the container near the card that pictures the same quantity.

Extensions and Variations

- Use picture cards (see page 13 for more information on picture cards) instead of jars filled with objects. Picture cards can be made by gluing pictures or stickers in different quantities on tagboard or cardboard. These cards can then be sorted under the key cards according to quantity. Remember, however, that objects are more real to young children than pictures of them.

- Give each child in a group a set of jars containing the quantities 1 to 5. Hold up one of the key cards and ask, "Can you each show me a jar that has this many?" or "Can you show me a jar that has more/less than this one?"

- One child holds up a jar or key card and says, "Can you find a jar that has this many?" The second child selects a jar that matches the quantity and puts it next to the first child's container or key card. The children then switch roles.

- Children retrieve different quantities of objects from around the room and put them near the appropriate key cards. For example, someone might bring 3 blocks from the block area and put them under the 3-card. The child returns the objects when the activity is over.

- For children who can count without using the key cards, ask, "Can you show me the jar that has three?"

Concepts and Skills Being Learned

- Recognizing that quantities are separate from the objects they describe. In other words, 5 rice grains *do* logically go with 5 golf tees.

- Classifying objects into sets, using quantity as the sorting criterion. Long before this activity, children are able to sort by other, more concrete qualities, such as color. Quantity takes things to a more abstract level. It is the mind that sees the objects in the container as 5, not the eye.

- Understanding *more*, *less*, and *same* with quantities small enough to be recognized by sight, without having to count.

ADVICE COLUMN

Use these activities to observe rather than to teach. When we see children struggling, it's easy to want to jump in and help. Avoid the temptation to correct children's errors and mistaken ideas as soon as you notice them. Piaget warns us that adult explanation or direct instruction does little to help children understand their mistakes. When we intervene, their responses are usually disinterest, confusion or, worse yet, dislike.

Instead, strive to create what cognitive psychologists call *discrepant events* and what Piaget called *disequilibrium*. This is a state of temporary confusion in which children's old explanations don't seem to work as well as they used to. Such a state of puzzlement sets in motion curiosity, increased attention, ongoing experimentation, and higher-order thinking—in other words, learning.

Consider this example: young children have a difficult time distinguishing quantity from volume. During the activities I've just described, children may hesitate to put a container of 3 cotton balls, which appears almost full, into the same category as a container of 3 rice grains, which appears almost empty. Yet each contains 3. It is only by working through this dilemma, with lots of hands-on matching and sorting and being free to make mistakes, that children eventually understand quantity as a concept.

Quantity Concentration

Materials and Setup

- ☐ 10 to 12 opaque bowls
- ☐ At least 30 small objects of various types and sizes, in quantities of 1 to 5. If the children are still at the stage of putting objects in their mouths, use larger objects
- ☐ Numeral cards (optional) (see page 13)

Basic Activity

1 To set up the game, place a single object under each of 2 overturned bowls, using a different object under each bowl.

2 Choose another 2 bowls and put 2 randomly selected objects under each of them. Continue in this pattern, until you have reached 5 objects.

3 With the bowls upside down and the objects hidden under them, the children shuffle the bowls into new positions.

4 The first child picks up one bowl, looks at the objects underneath, and then chooses another bowl to look under. If both bowls cover the same quantity of objects, the child turns the bowls upright, puts the objects in the bowls, and moves the pair in front of her.

5 Children take turns turning over bowls until all the bowls have been matched. If they wish, the children can then compare how many pairs each has found to determine the winner—but winning should not be emphasized as the reason for playing. Children play the game because it is fun.

Extensions and Variations

- Include 2 additional bowls with no objects under them. This introduces the concept of 0. Young children have a hard time accepting the absence of quantity as constituting quantity.

- For children who can count and know their numerals 0 to 5,
    - provide a set of numeral cards so the children can label their pairs with the appropriate number
    - for each set of bowls to be matched, place a numeral card under one bowl (for example, the 4-card) and the corresponding quantity of objects under the other (for example, 4 crayons). The children then match the quantity to the numeral

Concepts and Skills Being Learned

- Matching by quantity rather than by identity. Two bowls match only if they cover the same quantity of objects.

- Making a mental image of quantity for later recall. Children have to remember what quantity they have seen under the bowl rather than the objects themselves.

ADVICE COLUMN

Become comfortable with allowing children to decide if a match has been made. Learning comes when they notice and debate, not when we ensure that their answers are correct. At most, your intervention should involve asking them to take one more look at their choices. You might ask, "How can you show me that both bowls contain the same?" They might prove their answer by physically matching up each object in one set with each object in the other, in one-to-one fashion. You can ask older children, "So how many are under this one? And how many are under that one?" but again, if the children aren't yet at the counting stage, even this question oversteps your bounds.

In the end, if none of the participants is bothered by incorrect matches, let it go. When they find that the last two bowls don't match, they also discover an interesting puzzle to solve.

More-Less-Same Sorting I

Materials and Setup

☐ 24 picture cards showing quantities 1 to 8. There should be 3 cards for each quantity (see page 13 for more information)

☐ Key cards for numbers 3 to 6, showing either the numeral, the quantity, or both (see page 13 for more information)

☐ *More*, *less*, and *same* labels (see page 179 for a template)

Basic Activity

1 Children arrange the *less*, *same*, and *more* labels in order of quantity from left to right.

2 Children choose one of the key cards to put above the *same* label. This becomes the target quantity.

3 Children sort the picture cards under the appropriate label, according to whether the pictured quantity is more than, less than, or the same as the target quantity. For example, if the target quantity is 6, and the picture card shows 6 balloons, the card goes under the *same* label. If the pictured quantity is less than 6 (for example, 2 shoes), the card goes under the *less* label.

Extensions and Variations

Children find different sets of objects from the classroom that match the target quantity and put them under the *same* label, returning them afterward.

Concepts and Skills Being Learned

- Understanding that decisions about less and more must be made relative to an anchor number (for example, when the key card says 6, a picture card with 5 elephants goes in the *less* column. But if the key card is changed to 4, that same elephant card would go in the *more* column).

- Understanding that different quantities can go together under the *more* and *less* labels (for example, if the key card says 4, picture cards showing 5 bananas and 7 marbles would both be in the *more* column, because 5 and 7 are both more than 4).

- Becoming comfortable judging *more*, *less*, and *same* based on the quantity of objects, not on their attributes (for example, picture cards showing 2 elephants and 5 elephants do not necessarily belong in the same column).

ADVICE COLUMN

We use picture icons rather than symbols such as <, =, and > to label the categories. Doing so allows children who do not yet know their numerals or arithmetic symbols to perform the activities without help.

Again, let the children's choices stand. The point is for them to develop awareness of numbers, not for them to always be right. As children gain more of an understanding, their mistakes become fewer until they eventually disappear. It is more important to repeat an activity many times than to get it right the first time.

Dot Plates

Materials and Setup

- 15 or 20 plastic plates
- Colored dot stickers
- Key cards for numbers 1 to 5 (see page 13 for more information)
- Manipulatives to use as counters (optional)

Affix the colored dots in various patterns to the top side of the plate in quantities of 1 to 5. There should be 3 to 4 plates for each quantity. For example, the plates with 5 dots on them can display

- a classic arrangement of 5 dots, like that on a die or a playing card
- 5 dots in a straight line
- 2 red dots and 3 blue dots
- a square of 4 blue dots with 1 green dot off to the side

Basic Activity

1. Children lay out the key cards in numerical order, from left to right.

2. They sort the plates by appropriate key cards, according to quantity.

Extensions and Variations

- For children who do not know their number names yet,
    - show a plate quickly and then hide it. Ask, "Can you show me with these counters how many dots you saw?" or "Can you show me another plate with that many dots?"
    - use the plates for Quantity Concentration (see pages 21–22). Children turn all the plates upside down and take turns flipping over two plates at a time, trying to make a match.
- For children who know their number names,
    - show a plate quickly and then hide it. Ask, "How many dots did you see?"
    - introduce larger quantities (for example, 6 to 10), using color and physical arrangement to build on the patterned arrangements used on the 1 to 5 plates.

Concepts and Skills Being Learned

- A quantity can be divided in different ways without changing its total. For example, a plate with 4 blue dots and 1 red dot matches a plate with 3 green dots and 2 yellow dots. This is the beginning of part-whole awareness.

- Remembering that certain parts combine to make certain wholes. In other words, children begin to know without counting that 3 blue dots and 3 green dots on the plate make a total of 6 dots. It is important to appreciate what a significant leap this is. At this age, the quantity 6 is too large for young children to recognize visually. They can visually recognize the parts—in this example, two sets of 3—but the quantity 6 must be counted. So if children recognize 6 without counting it, then they must be remembering that 3 and 3 makes 6. In other words, they have memorized an addition fact.

ADVICE COLUMN

As children begin to associate number names with quantities, be sure to adjust your verbal prompts to their level of number-name awareness:

- **Level 1**—Children are able to put the plates in order and identify if one is more or less than another but don't yet know the name of the quantity. At this level, you can provide the number name that goes with the quantity they see (for example, "I see 4 dots."). When children are at this level (that is, they are still not sure what counting has to do with quantity), you mostly want to use the words *more, less,* and *the same* in talking with them, without mentioning numbers. When you do mention numbers, you are letting the children hear you using the number names rather than expecting them to know them.

- **Level 2**—Children know which number names go with which quantities when you say them (receptive language), but they are not yet confident enough to say the names themselves (expressive language). When you say the number name, these children can point to the appropriate quantity. At this level, you can say, "Which plate has 4 dots?"

- **Level 3**—Children can say the correct number name without assistance. At this level, you can say, "How many dots do you see on this plate?"

Mystery Bag Counting

Materials and Setup

- [ ] Mystery bag—an opaque bag or box into which children can reach and feel objects without seeing them
- [ ] A quantity of objects to place inside
- [ ] Counters (optional)
- [ ] Numeral cards (optional) (see page 13 for more information)

Design Note: Oatmeal boxes or shoe boxes with circular holes cut into both ends work well as mystery bags. Cut the feet off a pair of socks and attach the footless socks to the hole openings in the box, stuffing the socks inward. Children reach through the socks, one hand in each hole, to feel what's inside the container.

Basic Activity

1. The first child places a quantity of objects inside the mystery bag.

2. The second child reaches in the mystery bag and, without looking, says how many objects are inside.

3. The second child takes the objects out and together the children verify the quantity.

Extensions and Variations

- For children who may not know their number names yet,
  - the second child has a pile of 5 counters in front of her. After she reaches into the bag and feels the objects, she selects the number of counters from her pile that she thinks is the same as the quantity of objects in the mystery bag. **Note:** By using different objects for the mystery bag and for the counters, you encourage children to focus on matching quantities rather than matching objects.
  - have 6 mystery bags (paper lunch bags will do for this activity). Using an assortment of objects, place objects in quantities from 0 to 5 in each of the bags. Children try to put the bags in order from least to most by feeling how many objects are inside. When done, they can empty the bags to verify the order.
- For children who know their numerals,
  - the first child draws a numeral card that tells him how many objects to put in the mystery bag. After the second child has reached in and made her guess, the first child reveals the card.
  - play mystery bag addition, using a stack of numeral cards 1 through 3. The first child draws a numeral card from the stack and puts that many objects in the bag. The second child does the same. Looking at the two numerals, the children try to guess the total number of objects in the bag. They can then feel inside the bag and decide whether to change their guesses. They then pour out

the objects and reveal the actual sum. For more advanced counters, you can increase the range of numeral cards in the stack.

- play mystery bag subtraction, using two stacks of numeral cards. One stack should contain the numerals 4 to 6, while the other stack should contain the numerals 1 to 3. The first child draws a card from the first stack (4 to 6) and puts that many objects in the bag. The second child draws a card from the second stack (1 to 3) and takes that many objects *out* of the bag. Looking at the two numerals, the children try to guess how many objects are still in the bag. They both feel inside the bag and adjust their guesses if they wish. Then they empty out the bag and reveal the actual difference. For more advanced counters, you can increase the range of numeral cards in the stacks.

Concepts and Skills Being Learned

- Being able to visualize a quantity and to count by touch and not by sight. Practicing these skills broadens neural pathways used to recognize quantities.

- Being able to count a set of objects silently, without pointing to or moving the objects. This is a skill that children eventually have to master.

- The last two extensions help children start to develop an understanding of the part-whole concept, which is the early basis for addition and subtraction. If children have seen a quantity go into the mystery bag—say, 6 objects—and then see 2 objects come out, they need to somehow use those two numbers to conceptualize what is still in the bag. They may count the 2 objects they see and keep counting up to 6 to find the missing part of 6, or they may count 2 backward from 6 while they point to the objects removed from the bag. In the first case, they are adding parts to make the whole. In the second case, they are subtracting a part from the whole to find the missing part. In both cases, they are demonstrating that they see a relationship between the whole and its parts.

ADVICE COLUMN

Don't underestimate the importance of helping young children refine their sense of touch. Remember, not long ago these same children were putting everything into their mouths as a means of experiencing the world more fully. This age is ideal for building alternate brain pathways for experiencing the environment.

For some children, removing the visual stimulus by placing the items in the mystery bag has a calming and centering effect. Being able to name quantities without seeing them strikes most children as nothing short of magic.

Color-Quantity Bingo

Materials and Setup

☐ Bingo cards in a 4 x 4 configuration with red, green, yellow, and blue dots across the top and pictured quantities from 0 to 6 in the squares. You can find a template for these cards on page 180, but you'll need to fill in the squares with different arrangements of quantities on each card

☐ Set of 28 colored calling cards with pictured quantities. To make these cards, you can use red, green, yellow, and blue tagboard or use white tagboard with colored borders. For each color, add stickers or picture icons in quantities from 0 to 6 in different arrangements. The picture icons and their physical arrangement should not match those on the Bingo cards; this way, children's matches can be made only by quantity

☐ Lima beans or other counters to cover the squares that are called. Translucent Bingo chips work well because they keep the pictured quantities visible even after the square is covered

Basic Activity

1. The caller picks up a card and silently shows it to the other children or says, "This many under the red." Participants can examine or hold the calling card if they wish before deciding if they have a match. The caller should not refer to the quantity by name. **Note:** Children need to be reminded that they only have a match if their Bingo card matches the quantity *and* the color of the calling card. For example, if a *red* calling card shows 3 bears, they can't put a lima bean on the 3 balloons under the *blue* dot.

2. The game ends when one child has 4 in a row, when one of the children fills an entire card, or (the most common early childhood method) when *all* the children's cards are filled.

Extensions and Variations

- For children who can count, include quantities up to 10.

- For children who know their numerals, use numerals instead of pictures on the calling cards.

Concepts and Skills Being Learned

- Sets of different objects can be the same quantity.

- A quantity can be arranged many different ways and still be the same quantity.

- Making judgments based on two attributes. (Both the quantity *and* the color must be right for a match.)

ADVICE COLUMN

Avoid double-checking children's cards for accuracy. Mistakes are only important if other children notice and want to challenge them. In that case, let them debate each other, using whatever reasoning makes sense to them. Their conversation is perhaps the most educational part of the activity. You can ask questions and help children work through conflict, but do not decide for them what the right answer is.

If you want children to focus on matching by quantity, it's important that you don't give them a fallback strategy, such as matching by color, picture icon, or patterned arrangement of icons. For example, if children know they have a match because a picture shows elephants and they have elephants on their cards, they don't have to pay attention to how *many* elephants there are. In trying to help children feel more successful by using other cues, we may distract them from working on the target skill. Remember: the way to make children feel successful is not by making their practice error-free, but by making their errors risk-free.

Stand Up, Sit Down

Materials and Setup

None

Basic Activity

1. Have the children sit in a circle. As a group, decide on a target number.

2. Choose a child to stand in the center and be the pointer. The rest of the children remain seated. The child in the center walks around and points to the other children, one by one, while the group counts out loud from 1 up to the target number. The child who is pointed to when the target number is spoken stands up in place.

3. Counting begins again at 1, starting with the next child sitting down. Standing children are not counted. Each time the target number is reached, the child being pointed to stands up.

4. The game continues until everyone is standing. **Note:** This means that by the time the game is down to one child, that child is pointed to repeatedly until the target number is reached.

5. To extend the activity after all of the children are standing, the child in the center can switch to pointing to and counting the standing children. When the target number is reached, the child being pointed to sits down. The game continues until everyone is once again sitting.

Extensions and Variations

- Rather than having everyone in the group count together, the child being pointed to says the next number out loud. (Only do this if children are confident counters, and allow them to help each other when someone gets stuck.)

- Include backward counting in the game: count up to the target number and then back down to 0. In this version, the child being pointed to when the group says 0 stands up.

Concepts and Skills Being Learned

- Saying number names in proper sequence.

- One-to-one correspondence (for example, waiting to say the next number until the next child is pointed to—you'd be surprised how often children violate this rule).

- Stopping the count at a target number, even when there are more objects to be counted. This is another one of those rules that young children routinely break, and it's a very useful skill to have.

- Being able to count backward as well as forward. This skill is critical to developing a strong sense of the relationship of numbers to each other. Consider this: Wouldn't children develop a much stronger sense of alphabetical order if they learned to sing the Z-Y-X song as well as the A-B-C song?

ADVICE COLUMN

Don't choose too high a target number too soon. Let the group experience success and develop confidence. Gradually increase the target number as a challenge to the children, saying, "Okay, today I'm going to make it *really* hard." Children enjoy proving to you how smart they are.

Be careful to let the children do the counting. If your voice is too prominent, they listen to and shadow you instead of thinking of the next number themselves. That's both the drawback and the advantage of choral counting in general—it allows uncertain children to imitate rather than come up with their own response.

If an individual child is to say the next number, it's important to use what educators call *wait time*. Give each child time to come up with the answer, and be cautious about correcting any error. If the silence drags on too long, it's okay to give the child a hint (for example, holding up the appropriate number of fingers, or counting out loud up to the desired number and then pausing). Another useful technique is to let children know that they can point to a peer to provide the answer, if they want to. (This is similar to the phone-a-friend or poll-the-audience option used on some game shows.)

Let's Count Together

Materials and Setup

None

Basic Activity

1 This activity can take place anytime during the course of a day. Two or more children who are working together (for example, stacking blocks, scooping beans into a container, bouncing a ball back and forth) can take turns saying the next count out loud. For example, if they are seeing how many times they can bounce a ball to each other without missing, the first child bounces the ball to the second child, who catches it and says, "One." The ball is bounced back to the first child, who then says, "Two," and so on until they miss, at which point they start again. Or, in building a tower with blocks, one child places his block and says, "One," a second child sets her block on top and says, "Two," etc.

Extensions and Variations

When children are trying to achieve a personal best by comparing their results with previous attempts, an adult can assist them in recording their counts. Explore different ways of keeping track, such as tallying marks on a whiteboard, writing the score in numerals, or creating stacks of counters (older children can group their counters in sets of 10).

Concepts and Skills Being Learned

- The *cardinality* principle, which states that the last number said in a count names the quantity. For example, if children are counting 5 blocks, they say, "One, two, three, four, five." The last number that they say, 5, identifies how many blocks there are.

- The ability to pick up the count from a starting point other than the number 1. Note that each child has to say the next number without having personally said the number before. Eventually, as they learn to manipulate numbers mentally, children master counting forward or backward from any given starting point.

ADVICE COLUMN

Young children tend to count out loud together rather than only when it is their turn. Help them take pride in demonstrating their ability to count this harder way—one at a time, back and forth. You can also show them how to give their partner hints, such as making the sound the next number starts with. This discourages them from counting for their partner and supports better number sense for both children.

Hand Game I for a GROUP of children

Materials and Setup

☐ Supply of small blocks or other manipulatives. The objects should be large enough to be easily visible from a distance, but small enough that up to 5 items can fit in a child's closed fist. The objects can be all different or all the same

☐ Vinyl or cloth place mats (optional)

☐ Numeral cards (optional) (see page 13 for more information)

Basic Activity

1 Children gather in a circle.

2 Go around the circle with the container of manipulatives, giving the children between 1 and 5 objects to hold in their closed fists. Or the children can have place mats in front of them, under which they hide their items.

3 Select a child to begin. The child opens her hand or lifts her mat. The child sitting to the right of her says, "I see [*name the quantity*]. Do you agree?" The children then state aloud whether they agree or disagree ("We agree." or "We disagree."). To finish the turn, the child holding the items points to the objects one at a time while the group counts them out loud together.

4 Continue around the circle, moving counterclockwise until everyone has had a turn.

Extensions and Variations

• A simpler version of the game does not require each child in the circle to be a confident counter. As a child opens her fist, the group says in chorus: "We see [*name the quantity*]. Do you agree?" The child agrees or disagrees with a shake of the head, and the group counts the set out loud together.

• A more difficult version of the game requires children to make judgments of *relative* quantity. After a child reveals his quantity, the next child says, "I have more/less/the same. I have [*name the quantity*]. Do you agree?" The rest of the class can disagree if they feel the child is mistaken.

• After the quantities have been distributed, children get up and find other children who have the same quantity. Children stand in like-quantity groups and share their group's items and quantities ("I have 3 crayons. . . . I have 3 beans. . . . I have 3 paper clips. . . .") with the rest of the class.

• For children who know their numerals, place a pile of numeral cards in the center of the circle. After a child reveals her quantity, the child who is guessing retrieves the numeral card she thinks matches the quantity and places the card in front of the child whose quantity was revealed. The child whose quantity was revealed then says, "Yes, I have [*the quantity*]," or "No, I don't have [*the quantity*]."

Concepts and Skills Being Learned

- Associating a count with a visual quantity.

- The *cardinality* principle (for example, if a child counts "one, two, three, four, five," then the quantity is five). This is not intuitive to the young child. It is discovered with time and experience.

- Relating number names to more-less-same judgments.

ADVICE COLUMN

Make sure the objects you use are large enough for children to see without leaving their place. The goal of this activity is to connect children's sense of visual quantity with their sense of number. Notice that they are being asked to name the quantity without being able to touch or point to the individual items—a big step for some children.

Tug-of-War

for
TWO
or **MORE**
children

Materials and Setup

☐ A rectangular strip of tagboard marked off in 21 squares arranged in a straight line. The middle (eleventh) square should be marked with a colored dot

☐ One teddy bear counter (or some other attractive manipulative)

☐ One standard die, with dots 1 to 6

Basic Activity

1 Two children sit opposite each other, positioning the game strip between them so that the marked square is directly in front of them and the other squares extend to their left and to their right. The bear starts out on the center square.

2 The children take turns rolling the die and moving the bear the number of spaces to their right that the die indicates. They are basically pulling the bear in opposite directions with each toss of the die.

3 The game ends when the bear falls off one end of the game strip or the other.

4 The children return the bear to the center square and start again.

Extensions and Variations

- Make a die for the children that has 0 to 5 dots rather than 1 to 6. Or children can use a spinner instead of a die. Or if children are comfortable with numerals, they can use a die with numerals rather than dots. (See page 164 for directions on how to make your own dice or spinners.)

- Add a second die and let both children roll at the same time. They must figure out which number is bigger and move the bear in the right direction after noting the difference between the 2 rolls. For example, if one child rolls a 5, and the other a 2, the first child moves the bear 3 spaces in her direction. Note that this game combines the effects of 2 turns into 1.

- Confident counters can use a longer tug-of-war strip and roll 2 dice, with each child moving the teddy bear the combined number of dots. Other variations include using 1 die with dots

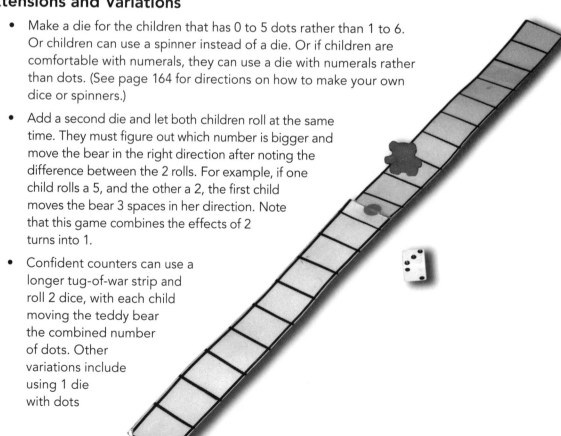

and 1 with numerals, or 2 with numerals. Or they can spin a 3-to-9 spinner, and subtract the number rolled on a 1-to-3 die. Children are limited only by your imagination and their own skill levels.

Concepts and Skills Being Learned

This is a deceptively complex activity. Many skills are practiced in this board game.

- Recognizing the quantity on the die and translating it into a number of jumps.

- Learning that the square the bear sits on at the start of each round is 0 and not 1 in the count. In other words, the starting square does not get counted. Young children often have trouble with this part of moving a fixed number of spaces, routinely moving one space fewer than they should.

- Noticing how the bear's relative position changes from one turn to the next. For example, if the first child rolls a 4 and the second child rolls a 6, the bear moves 2 spaces closer to the second child's end. This is a hands-on way of experiencing the relative size of numbers.

- Anticipating what number is needed on the next turn to end the game, or knowing where the bear is going to end up after a roll, even before counting. Note that the center square and end squares are particularly useful anchors around which this awareness develops. For example, if the bear is two squares to the left of the center square and the child rolls a 4, he may notice that 2 of the 4 will bring him to the center square and that his total move will put him 2 squares on the other side of that. He may not be able to articulate his awareness that 2 + 2 = 4, but he is developing an understanding of this important part-whole concept.

- Some of the extensions above build additional skills, such as recognizing numerals, associating numerals with quantities, counting on, adding, and subtracting.

ADVICE COLUMN

If children want to keep track of wins and losses, they can do so by tallying, drawing from a pile of counters, or stamping bears on a strip of paper under their names. However, in most cases preschoolers don't care about keeping track of their wins, and if that's the case, don't suggest to them they ought to do so. The joy should be in the activity, not in the winning.

Store

for
ONE
or MORE
children

Materials and Setup

- One suit of playing cards, numbers 2 to 10, plus the ace (which for this game is 1). Cover the numerals in the corners with whiteout. Or make your own cards without numerals, using stickers on tagboard

- Small container to use as a shopping basket

- Sorting tray, kept on a classroom shelf, with different types of attractive objects, such as buttons, wooden beads, smooth stones, or small, multicolored pom-poms; this is the store

Basic Activity

1. The child shuffles the deck and sets it on the table or rug, face down.

2. The child then picks one card. This is the first shopping list. The child's task is to remember how many items to shop for. Give the child a few moments to study the card. You might say, "Bring back exactly this many items from the store—no more, and no less. Exactly this many."

3. The child takes the shopping basket to the store, leaving the shopping list behind on the table or rug. This aspect is critical—the child must remember how many things to shop for, rather than match objects to the list at the store.

4. The child brings back the selections from the store and lays them out with the shopping list. Often the child chooses to place the objects on the card itself, covering each icon with an object, and then taking back any extras or retrieving any more that are needed. To support a child who is checking his answer, you can point to the card and ask, "How can you prove to me that you brought back exactly this many?"

5. Repeat this activity with the next shopping list in the deck. When the child has gone through all the cards in the deck, she can use the shopping basket to return the objects to the sorting tray, putting them in their appropriate compartments.

Extensions and Variations

- For younger children, limit the cards used to 1 to 5.
- For more confident counters,
  - create shopping lists that contain more dots
  - create shopping lists on which the dots do not constitute a recognizable pattern
  - create cards whose dots are too small and close together for the child to be able to place objects on top of them to check his solutions

Concepts and Skills Being Learned

- Forming a mental representation of a quantity. Since children can't take the shopping list along to the store, they have to devise a strategy for remembering how many things to get.

- Making judgments of more-less-same. In this activity, children make judgments about the quantity on the card compared to the number of items they brought back from the store. "Did I bring enough? Did I bring too many?"

- Understanding part-whole relationships. The patterns of the icons on the playing cards allow children to see the larger quantities in terms of manageable parts. For example, the 9-card can be visualized as two 4s plus 1 more. This allows even children who can't count yet to successfully play this game.

- Using 1-to-1 correspondence. The easiest version of the game uses objects small enough to be placed on top of the shopping-list icons, matching one object to each icon on the card. When the dots on the cards are too small and close together for the objects to fit, children must develop alternate strategies for deciding if they have brought back the same quantity as on the card.

- Estimating. Children who can't count yet form an impression of larger quantities as *a lot*. Comparing the number of objects they bring back to the number of icons on the cards helps them fine-tune their sense of approximate quantity.

- Classifying. Children return the items to their appropriate compartment at the end of the game, classifying them by type.

ADVICE COLUMN

I've found it's better not to use pictures for icons on the shopping lists. They confuse children unnecessarily; they may believe that the pictured item is what they need to find at the store. Even color can be distracting—some children may limit themselves to finding objects that match the colors of the dots on the cards. Never underestimate how much young children's logic is grounded in their senses.

If the quantity the child brings back does not match the shopping list, you can ask useful questions, such as,

- "Did you bring too many or too few?"

- "What can you do about these?" (Point to the leftover objects or the uncovered dots.)

- "Which one has fewer than the other?" "Which one has more than the other?"

- "How many more/fewer objects do you need?"

Showdown

for **TWO** or **MORE** children

Materials and Setup

☐ Two decks of playing cards with the face cards removed (that is, 80 cards, ace to 10). White out the numerals in the corners. You can also make your own cards without numerals by using stickers on tagboard

Basic Activity

1 Children divide the deck of cards into approximately equal piles.

2 The players each turn over one card from their piles simultaneously. The child who has the card showing the largest quantity takes the trick. If there is a tie for highest card, the children who tie then turn over their next card to see who takes the trick.

Extensions and Variations

- A child who doesn't want to play the game can still use this deck of playing cards by laying matching quantities of counters onto or next to each of the cards. Or the child can sort and sequence the cards from 1 to 10.

- Make your own set of playing cards and affix the icons irregularly. This forces more counting on the children's part and helps them develop strategies for counting messy sets.

- Let the children make their own classroom card set using stamps, stickers, or markers.

- Change the rules so the child who has the smaller quantity takes the trick. Or use a more/less spinner so that for each trick, the spinner determines whether the high card or low card takes the trick. See page 164 for information on how to make a spinner.

- Change the rules and include a bowl of counters. The object of the game is to acquire counters. When the trick is played, the child with the larger quantity takes from the bowl the number of counters equal to the difference between the card values. For example, if the first child's card is a 6 and the second child's card is a 4, the first child would take 2 counters from the bowl. If you wish, you can provide each child with a game card (for example a 5 x 10 configuration of squares) on which to place counters as they acquire them. In this last version, the game ends when one child fills her card.

- For younger children, use only cards 1 to 5.

- For children who know their numerals, make playing cards that have only numerals on them. Here, the judgment of "Who has more?" must be made by using number sense, not by comparing quantities visually (for example, "I have a 9 and you have a 7, and 9 is a bigger number than 7.")

Concepts and Skills Being Learned

- Starting to move from a visual sense of quantity to counting. The higher playing cards are harder to identify and compare using the visual (*subitizing*) recognition system.

- Seeing part-whole relationships. For example, children notice that the 8 has 2 rows of 4, and that the 9 has the same 2 rows of 4 with 1 more in the middle.

- Making judgments of more-less-same. Children need lots of practice with this. For a long time, they can know that one quantity is 7 and another quantity is 9, yet still not have a clue about which set is more. They fall back on their visual sense (that is, which one looks like more) to make this judgment, whether they've counted the sets or not. Knowing that 9 is more than 7 comes later.

- The last extension includes comparing numbers at the symbolic level (comparing numerals rather than comparing quantities of objects) and judging the size of the difference between numbers (for example, "How many more dots does this card have than that card?").

ADVICE COLUMN

Don't suggest to children that they count and then compare numbers as the appropriate solution strategy (for example, "You have 7, and you have 9. So who has more?"). This approach makes no sense to children at the early stages of number sense for reasons I've described above. Instead, encourage the children to share their reasoning with each other. A child may say, "Look, I have this many over here and this many over here, and you only have that many and that many. So I have more." You can also suggest that the children look at a number line to see which number is further to the right. (A number line is a strip of paper showing numerals in order, in this case, from 1 to 10.)

Pay attention to which children tend to use counting as a solution strategy without prompting from adults. Such counting is a good indicator that these children are ready to move on to more sophisticated explorations of numbers.

Race to 20

Materials and Setup

☐ Game board—a 4 x 20 configuration of squares (to accommodate up to 4 players) on tagboard, with a start line and finish line marked at either end. You can make your own board with a horse race or car race theme, or you can use the racetrack template on page 181. However, the racetrack template only goes up to 10, so you will want to use a die or spinner numbered from 1 to 3.

☐ Game pieces; these can be any small manipulatives, as long as each piece is different

☐ A die or spinner numbered from 1 to 6 (See page 164 for directions on how to make your own dice or spinners.)

Basic Activity

1 Players take turns rolling the die and moving that many spaces forward. Play continues until all the players have crossed the finish line.

Extensions and Variations

• Use a die or spinner with 0 to 5 dots or picture icons. For very young children, use a die showing 1 to 3 dots (each number appears twice on this die, with opposite faces showing the same number).

• For children who know their numerals, use a numeral die or spinner.

• Make a circular racetrack divided into 10 segments. The children decide at the beginning of each game how many laps to play, or they simply play till they lose interest in the game. Provide counters to help the children keep track of their completed laps.

Concepts and Skills Being Learned

- Translating the quantity on the die or spinner into the appropriate number of jumps.

- Treating the square currently occupied as 0. In other words, the count doesn't begin until after the first jump. It takes a while for children to get the hang of this.

- Quantifying the position of the child's game piece compared to other pieces in the race and to the finish line. For example, if the first child is 4 spaces in the lead, and her opponent rolls a 5, the first child now finds herself 1 space behind. Meanwhile, the third child, who is 3 spaces from the finish line, sees that he needs to roll a 4 or better to win.

- Practice using *ordinal numbers*. Ordinal numbers are used to describe order or position, such as being first, second, or third, to cross the finish line.

- Early experiences with probability. Children may hope to roll a particular number, or ponder whether a certain player, game piece, color, column, etc. is the lucky one. Even adults have a hard time figuring out what's predictable and what's simply random.

ADVICE COLUMN

There is back-and-forth debate in the educational community about using competitive games with young children. My personal opinion is that the competitive spirit is a natural and healthy part of being human and a powerful motivator to participate. It is also one of the reasons people engage in activity with others rather than alone. Our goal should be to influence how children react to winning or losing, not to eliminate all competition from their world. We must teach them to be gracious winners and resilient losers and to take more pleasure in the activity than in the victory. Upon completing an enjoyable activity, children's natural tendency is to repeat the activity, not to obsess over the outcome. Keep repetition as their goal.

Graphing Mats and Voting Boxes

for ONE or MORE children

Materials and Setup

☐ Graphing or sorting materials (see "Extensions and Variations" below for the materials needed to make them)

Basic Activity

1 Voting occurs frequently in the classroom—for example, what book to read next, whether to go outside or stay in, how many people should be able to use the reading corner at a time. You can also take a poll surveying hair color, number of siblings, number of family pets, or children's birth month. When children vote for preferences or take a poll, give them materials such as those listed below to create a visual representation (that is, a graph) of their responses. These graphing materials help the children line up items side-by-side so that they're spaced equally in straight columns. Such an arrangement helps children make visual comparisons of quantities. Children need help remembering to place one object per space under the appropriate label.

2 For children who do not yet read, it is best to label columns using picture icons in place of (or in addition to) written labels.

3 Once children have sorted out and lined up the materials, they can visually compare the lengths of the columns to see which category contains more. Children who can count can determine how many items are in each column, how many more objects one column contains than another, and how many items there are all together.

Extensions and Variations

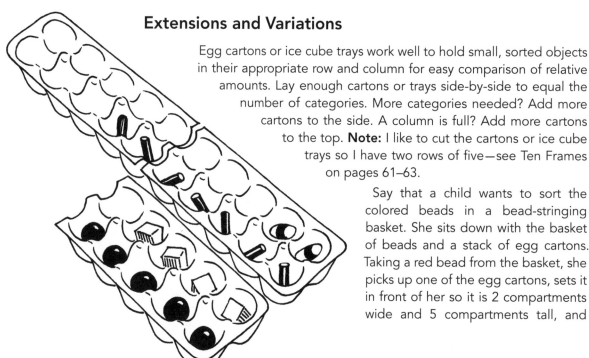

Egg cartons or ice cube trays work well to hold small, sorted objects in their appropriate row and column for easy comparison of relative amounts. Lay enough cartons or trays side-by-side to equal the number of categories. More categories needed? Add more cartons to the side. A column is full? Add more cartons to the top. **Note:** I like to cut the cartons or ice cube trays so I have two rows of five—see Ten Frames on pages 61–63.

Say that a child wants to sort the colored beads in a bead-stringing basket. She sits down with the basket of beads and a stack of egg cartons. Taking a red bead from the basket, she picks up one of the egg cartons, sets it in front of her so it is 2 compartments wide and 5 compartments tall, and places the bead in the bottom position closest to her. When she finds more red spheres, she continues filling the spaces above the red one. Her attention now shifts to blue cubes, so she places one in the bottom position of the next column, and all the other blue cubes go above that. She finds 8 of them, and when she gets to the sixth blue cube, she gets another egg carton and puts it above the first so she can continue adding cubes. When she turns her attention to the blue spheres, she grabs another egg carton and places it alongside the first to create a new category. Note that the child decides for herself if she has a new category. If the red spheres and the red cylinders seem the same to her, she can put them in the same column.

Floor graphing mats

Take a large vinyl mat, such as an old vinyl window shade or shower curtain, and lay it on the floor. Using masking tape or a permanent marker, create a square grid, with rows and columns marked off.

Floor mats are good for sorting large objects and for whole-group work. I've used them, for example, in a circle activity in which children take off one of their shoes and toss it into the middle of the circle. Then we decide how we are going to sort them (for example, left shoes versus right shoes, brown shoes versus white shoes) and proceed to arrange them on the mat in sorted columns, placing one shoe in each square of the grid. I may write the words *left* and *right* on index cards and put the cards at the base of the mat to label each category.

Voting boxes or pins

Voting materials can be personalized with children's names and pictures. Children can decorate their own voting piece, if they wish.

Some examples of these personalized voting materials:

- Magnetic rectangles—these can be made using tagboard cut into rectangles with magnetic strips attached to the back. Have the children personalize their own magnetic rectangle. The children then attach their personalized rectangles to metal cookie sheets or a magnetized whiteboard when voting. You can even buy paint at the hardware store that magnetizes any surface you choose. Children can then place their voting piece above the appropriate category and visually compare the heights of various columns. For example, they can attach their rectangles to a prepared chart to indicate which center they plan to work in first following circle time or to indicate who was their favorite character in the story read to them that day.

- Clothespins—create personalized clothespins by writing children's names on them and having children decorate them. To vote, they attach the clothespins to ropes, ribbons, or yarn hung vertically or horizontally. For example, they can move their clothespins as they arrive each day at the program from a ribbon labeled *absent* to a ribbon labeled *present*. The class can then count how many children are absent and how many children are present that day.

- One-pint milk cartons—thoroughly wash a set of empty one-pint milk cartons. Flatten the tops, cover the cartons with construction paper, and let children decorate them or glue a small photo of themselves to the carton. For voting, they can stack the cartons on top of each other on a window ledge or the railing of a whiteboard. What results is a great three-dimensional bar graph. If children vote for their favorite way of eating corn, it's easy for them to see that, say, more children like corn on the cob than creamed corn.

Voting materials can be stored in a basket when not in use.

Concepts and Skills Being Learned

- Numbers are useful in many aspects of our lives.

- Relative quantity.

- In these activities, children are creating object graphs or concrete graphs. These represent the first stage of becoming familiar with how to read graphs. Eventually children need to be able to interpret graphs in which icons or colored-in squares are used instead of actual objects. In the meantime, they are producing visual displays that answer questions they find personally meaningful and important.

ADVICE COLUMN

Try making voting materials with children's pictures on them. Young children don't like being reduced to mere data points. They like to know which one they are on the graph and which one is their best friend.

Realize that children have different ideas about what constitutes a new category than adults do. For example, you may think that milk and chocolate milk or french fries and hash browns belong to the same category, but children may view them as distinct categories. Go with their rationale.

Counting throughout the Day

There are many opportunities for children to count throughout the day as they observe, record, or sort quantities. To continue practicing and applying the skills discussed in this section, children can

- count as part of indoor play (how many blocks they can stack before a tower falls, how many flowers they draw in their picture)

- help set a table with the appropriate number of place settings

- pick out a certain number of grocery items in the role-playing area

- count the number of items each child gets for snack

- sing and act out number songs, poems, and finger plays

- clap the syllables in their names or in other words of interest

- listen to number-related stories. Adults should frequently ask number-related questions during reading time, such as, "I wonder which picture has more bears in it?"

- practice dialing a telephone number in the role-playing area

- count possessions or personal collections of objects

- use a calendar, noticing the numbers on it, the number of days until an important event, etc.

- compare birthdays or how old they are in relation to other members of their family

- count coins

- count steps, jumps, number of turns taken

- march and clap rhythms with different numbers of beats

- notice numbers at home and in the community (in stores, menus, street numbers, phone numbers, newspapers, ball players' jerseys)

- notice quantities while on a neighborhood walk (the number of windows in a house, the number of trees in a yard, the number of birds in a tree). On occasion, this can be extended into a clipboard scavenger hunt for which children decide ahead of time what items to look for on their walk, and then have the teacher record a tally mark each time they spot an item

- gather materials during a nature walk (flower blossoms, leaf branches, acorn clusters). Later, they can count how many of each type they have gathered, or look closely at some other aspect of the objects gathered that involves quantity (the number of petals on a flower, the leaves per cluster on a stem, the seeds in a pod)

- count other aspects of interest while exploring the outdoor play area (the number of pill bugs under a rock, the number of worms on a square of sidewalk, the number of times they can dribble a ball or jump over a rope without missing)

Concepts and Skills Being Learned

- Numbers apply to many aspects of everyday life.

- Activities, events, and experiences can be classified by quantity (for example, sometimes you can hop 10 times on one foot before stumbling, sometimes only 6).

ADVICE COLUMN

Parents hear a lot these days about the importance of reading to their children every day. We need to be just as diligent in educating parents about the importance of pointing out quantity to their children in daily life.

Be careful of using closed questions in conversations that you have with children about quantity. Closed questions can be answered with a *yes* or *no*, or another single-word response. To young children, such questions feel like a mini-test that they either pass or fail. Instead, use more open-ended questions, such as "I wonder" ones: "There seem to be a lot of dolls in the crib. . . ." Pause, see if the child responds, and if not, then ask, "I wonder how many there are?" You can also ask more-less-same questions, such as "I wonder which of you has more grapes on your plate?" These types of questions give children more freedom to respond as they see fit and in ways that make sense to them.

However children respond, accept their answer rather than correct it. If you want them to reconsider their initial response, you can always respond in a personal rather than an authoritative fashion—for example, "Really? I thought there were 7." Children can choose to check and revise their response, or they can let it go as a difference of opinion. In either case, you have gathered valuable information about their current state of number sense, which was your intention in the first place.

The Literature Connection

ADVICE COLUMN

Stories are always a good stimulus to mathematical activity. The following books encourage children to relate to quantities rather than to numbers. Those that use numbers only go up to a small number, such as 5.

   Many of the books listed at the end of chapter 3 are also appropriate as read-alouds and interactive explorations for children who are beginning to count.

Anholt, Catherine, and Laurence Anholt. 1993. *One, Two, Three, Count with Me.* New York: Penguin Books.

Arenson, Roberta. 1998. *One, Two, Skip a Few! First Number Rhymes.* Kingswood, U.K.: Barefoot Books.

Babbitt, Natalie. 2001. *Elsie Times Eight.* New York: Hyperion.

Baker, Alan. 1998. *Little Rabbit's First Number Book.* New York: Laurouse Kingfisher Chambers.

Canizares, Susan, and Betsey Chessen. 1999. *How Many Can Play?* New York: Scholastic.

Christelow, Eileen. 1989. *Five Little Monkeys Jumping on the Bed.* New York: Clarion.

Koller, Lynn. 1999. *One Monkey Too Many.* Orlando, Fla.: Harcourt Brace.

Murphy, Stuart. 1997. *Just Enough Carrots.* New York: HarperCollins.

Nayer, Judy. 1996. *How Many?* New York: Newbridge.

———. 1998. *More or Less.* New York: Newbridge.

Novak, Matt. 2005. *Too Many Bunnies.* Brookfield, Conn.: Roaring Brook Press.

Riordan, James. 1998. *Little Bunny Bobkin.* Waukesha, Wis.: Little Tiger Press.

Weir, B. Alison. 1999. *The SunMaid Raisins Play Book.* New York: Simon & Schuster.

Williams, Sue. 1998. *Let's Go Visiting.* Orlando, Fla.: Harcourt Brace.

Wilson, Karma, and Joan Rankin. 2003. *A Frog in the Bog.* New York: Simon & Schuster.

3

counting to 10

When children work with quantities larger than 5 or 6, they can no longer be sure how many objects there are simply by looking at them. They must rely on counting. At this stage, identifying and comparing quantities depends on the knowledge "If I counted it, then I know how many there are" and "If I counted 2 sets, and they both contain the same number of objects, then they have the same quantity."

Chapter 3 provides plenty of activities that push children's counting skills up to 10. Ten is an obvious milestone, since our counting system is based on 10. That's also why I refer to 10 as an *anchor number* in children's counting (as is 5, which is half of 10—and the number of fingers on one hand). Several of the activities in chapter 3 prepare children for the place-value work they will do much later in school (for example, knowing that 47 is four 10s and seven 1s).

In chapter 3's activities, children also learn to practice counting backward from 10. This skill helps them develop more flexible counting strategies, as well as discovering that quantities can be taken apart and reassembled without affecting the final count. This concept will be explored more fully in chapter 6.

Some of the activities in this chapter require commercial sets of Montessori equipment, available from one of the many Montessori materials distributors. Go to the Montessori Foundation's Web site, www.montessori.org, and find Suppliers—Montessori Materials; this offers you a list to choose from. Hello Wood Products (www.hellowood.com) makes some good handmade materials. I also supply you with instructions for making homemade alternatives to the commercial products.

Essentially, if the way I describe a set of materials is intimidating, don't bypass the activity. Be creative, and find other materials that will accomplish the same goals.

You'll know children should be working with activities in chapter 3 if

- they stumble with counting sets beyond 5 or 6, especially if the objects are not arranged in a straight line

- the size or arrangement of objects still confuses their sense of how many there are

- when told 2 sets have different numbers of objects (for example, 1 set has 6, the other has 8), they still are not sure which one has more

Number Rods

Materials and Setup

☐ Fifteen rods cut from wood, 2.5 cm wide x 2.5 cm high (1 x 1 inch) marked in decimeter (dm) increments of length. Paint the rods in alternating 1 dm units of red and blue. **Note:** 1 decimeter = 10 centimeters, or approximately 4 inches. Two and a half cm is approximately 1 inch, so in English units, the rods are approximately 1 x 1 inch with painted increments 4 inches in length. The exact number and specifications of the rods are

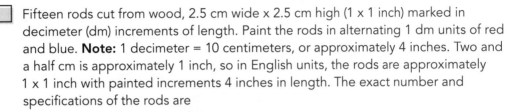

- Two 1 dm (4 inch) rods, one red (R) and one blue (B)
- Two 2 dm (8 inch) rods, both with a R-B sequence
- Two 3 dm (12 inch) rods, one R-B-R, the other B-R-B
- Two 4 dm (16 inch) rods, both R-B-R-B
- Seven 5 dm (20 inch) rods, six of them R-B-R-B-R, one B-R-B-R-B

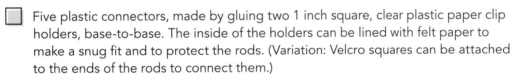

Note: This is a variation on a standard piece of Montessori equipment, which has 10 rods, 1 dm to 1 m in length with segments in alternating R-B sequence. You also can use a commercial set of number rods for this activity, taking out the 6 dm through 1 m rods.

☐ Five plastic connectors, made by gluing two 1 inch square, clear plastic paper clip holders, base-to-base. The inside of the holders can be lined with felt paper to make a snug fit and to protect the rods. (Variation: Velcro squares can be attached to the ends of the rods to connect them.)

Alternatives

- Flat versions of the number rods can be made using tagboard or wood slats and the dimensions and colors specified above. However, three-dimensional pieces are sturdier and more real to the children.

- You can also make a high-quality, durable set of number rods from lengths of half-inch PVC pipe. White PVC pipe is available in any plumbing outlet and is inexpensive, easy to cut, and can be colored with permanent markers. You can use three-quarter-inch PVC connector pieces as the rod connectors (I lined the inside of the connectors with felt paper to make a snugger fit. You can also place Velcro strips on the ends of the rods, as shown in the photo on the next page).

- Consider starting with your classroom block set: If you treat the unit block as a 2, the half-block becomes a 1 and the double block a 4. You'll need someone with a table saw to make your 3- and 5-rods (and others, if you want to go up to 10), but

it's a nice way of helping your children experience the block set in a new way. You can use the blocks as they are, use a pencil line to show the unit segments, or use a colored wood stain and polyurethane sealer to make red and blue segments.

- You can even make a number rod set using cardboard tubes cut to the lengths listed on the previous page. You can cover them with alternating red and blue construction paper, and then wrap with clear contact paper to protect and make them more rigid. *These tend not to be very durable.*

Note: There has been some discussion among Montessori folk, especially those dealing with children who have special needs, about red and blue being too harsh a color contrast for some children to process. The solution? Replace the blue with white or some other neutral color.

Basic Activity

1. Put the rods that are blue on both ends to the side. Children start with the remaining rods randomly distributed.

2. Children find and count one 1-rod, and then a 2-rod, and so on, placing them in ascending order, staircase-style. The segments aligned on the left should all be red.

3. To make 6, they choose another 5-rod and the blue 1-rod, and count: "One, two, three, four, five . . . six," using the connector to hold the two pieces together.

4. Children continue until they have assembled all 10 rods.

Extensions and Variations

- Adults can play various name games with the children:

    - "Who has a _____ (3-rod, etc.)?"

    - "Where is the _____ ?"

    - "Which one is missing?"

    - "I have five. What do I need to make eight?"

- To add an additional counting dimension to the rods, children can place tiles or other manipulatives on top of each of the colored sections as they count the rod. For example, they might take the 4-rod, place a tile on the left-most section and count "One . . . ", place a tile on the next section and say "Two . . .", etc. After placing all the tiles, they can go back and point to each tile in sequence, counting: "One . . . two . . . three . . . four."

- Children can build the rods in other patterned arrangements, such as

    - a maze spiraling inward. In other words, place the 9-rod on the end of the 10-rod so that it's perpendicular; the 8-rod at the end of the 9-rod but again perpendicularly, and so on. (See illustration below.)

    - a vertical staircase or pyramid by placing the number rods on top of each other with the largest at the bottom.

    - an abstract fir tree, using alternating vertical and horizontal arrangements—in other words, place the 10-rod horizontally to form the lowest branches, the 9-rod vertically and centered to form the trunk, the 8-rod horizontally, the 7-rod vertically, etc., with the 1-rod sitting vertically at the top of the tree. The tree can even be decorated afterward, using other classroom manipulatives. As an added challenge, encourage the children to place their decorations in other patterned or symmetrical arrangements. (See illustration on next page.)

    - an 11-unit x 5-unit rectangle by placing the 1-rod on the end of the 10-rod to form the first row (10 + 1 = 11), the 2-rod on the end of the 9-rod to form the second row (9 + 2 = 11), and so on until there are five rows.

- Children can use the number rods laid end to end to measure aspects of the room or the outdoor environment.

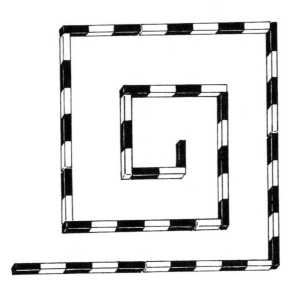

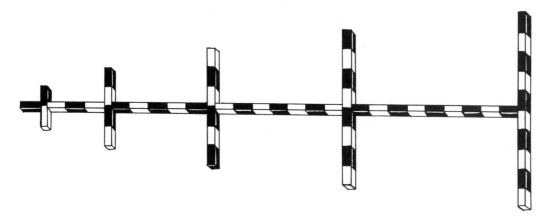

Concepts and Skills Being Learned

- Five and 10 as anchor numbers (for example, 7 is 5 and 2 more), with 10 equaling two 5s. This is one of the most important early number principles for children to discover, laying the groundwork for an understanding of the place value system. The rod design parallels the way children do much of their early counting—using the fingers of their own two hands.

- Counting accurately to 10. The length of the rods serves as a control of error. If children miscount a rod, the lengths do not increase in a proper stair-step fashion.

- Counting on. Having children make the 6-rod using the 5-rod plus 1 more encourages the child to count "Five . . . six" rather than "One, two, three, four, five . . . six."

- Cardinality principle—that is, the last number counted names the rod.

Cuisenaire Rods

Materials and Setup

☐ Commercial set of Cuisenaire rods. Cuisenaire rods are a set of small, color-coded wooden or plastic rods, ranging from 1 to 10 units in length. Cuisenaire rods have the advantage of being color coded, so the child can learn the quantities by sight. The 1-rod is a 1 cm (.4 inch) cube. The 10-rod is 1 dm (4 inches) long. Cuisenaire rods aren't very expensive and are probably worth acquiring if you don't already have them. You can purchase these from almost any early childhood catalog. You can also buy rubber stamps to stamp versions of the rods on paper. These stamps open up a whole new realm of possibilities for classroom activities and materials-making

Alternatives

- Modify the set by marking off one side of each rod in unit increments, using permanent markers. For example, draw 4 lines across one of the faces of the 5-rod, dividing the length into 5 unit increments (see illustration). The other faces should be left blank so children will still think of the rod holistically as 5. (See the "Counting On" activity under "Extensions and Variations" below for an example of how this distinction becomes important.)

- If you don't have a set of Cuisenaire rods, you can use any material that can be cut into different lengths and color coded (plastic straws, craft sticks, tagboard). You can use any 10 colors to represent the different lengths. For smaller hands, consider increasing the dimensions (in fact, some early childhood catalogs carry larger versions of the Cuisenaire rods).

Basic Activity

1 Children identify the different quantities by color. If you have marked one side of the rods in unit increments, they can also count the units to verify their answers.

Extensions and Variations

- Adults can play various naming games with the children:
    - "Who has the _____ (6-rod, etc.)?"
    - "Where is the _____?"
    - "Which one is missing?"
    - "I have five. What do I need to make eight?"
- "Counting On." A child chooses a rod, identifies it (for example, 5-rod), and places it on the table with the marked increments facing down. Another child adds another rod to the end, this time with the marked increments facing up. Together, the

children try to guess what the combined amount is. (**Note:** They should try to do this without turning over the first rod: "Five… six, seven, eight. Eight.") To verify their guess, they can turn over the first rod so all the increments are showing and they can count the total.

- "More or Less?" Two children each pull a rod from an opaque bag, identify them, and spin a More/Less spinner to decide whether the child with more or the child with less wins (see page 164 for suggestions on how to buy or make spinners). The child with more or less figures out how many more or less his rod is (placing the rods side-by-side is the most common strategy), and he adds that many counters to his pile. Players continue pulling rods and scoring points until they reach a target amount or they tire of the game.

- "How Else Can You Make _____ ?" One child selects a rod or a pair of rods. Another child constructs the same length using other rods.

- "Go Fish." For this game, you need 3 or more children and 40 rods (that is, 4 of each type). Each child starts with 4 rods and hides them behind a small screen. The rest of the rods are kept in an opaque bag. The object of the game is to collect as many sets of 4 matching rods as possible. To begin the game, one child looks at her rods and asks another child if he has a specific rod: "Zach, do you have any [name a number]s?" If the child has any of that type of rod, he gives those rods to the first child. If he doesn't have any of that type, he says, "Go fish," and the first child selects a rod from the bag. The next child then takes a turn. When a child has collected all 4 of a particular type, she can lay them off to the side as her trick. The children continue until all the rods have been matched into sets.

Concepts and Skills Being Learned

- Experiencing quantities both discretely (as countable units) and holistically (as a whole amount).

- Relative quantity.

- Counting on, counting back.

- Part-whole relationships.

ADVICE COLUMN

Cuisenaire rods are useful because they tie a color to a specific quantity. For the beginning counter, however, the fact that the rods are not marked off in increments makes them uncountable. Marking unit increments on one side of the rods adds this needed feature to the materials and makes them much more user-friendly for children who are only beginning to count.

Decimeter Rods

CONSTRUCTION REQUIRED

for TWO or MORE children

Materials and Setup

- ☐ Fifty-five rods cut from wood, 2.5 cm wide x 2.5 cm high x 1 dm long (1 inch x 1 inch x 4 inches). Paint 30 of the rods red and 25 of them blue. This set is basically a cut-up version of the number-rod set from pages 53–56. What you are making is 55 1-rods, with colors to match all the segments of your 1 to 10 number-rod set

- ☐ Carrying tray or basket

- ☐ The number-rod set (see pages 53–56)

Alternatives

- Use the template on page 182 to make decimeter rods out of tagboard according to the above specifications, or use any of the materials listed under "Alternatives" on pages 53–54 in the number-rod activity.

- You can also buy decimeter rods, although the only Montessori materials manufacturer I've found who makes them is Hello Wood Products (www.hellowood.com).

Basic Activity

1. A child has the number rods on one side of the room, and another child has the decimeter rods on the other side.

2. The first child holds up one of the number rods for the second child to see and says, "Can you bring me what you need to make this?"

3. The second child chooses the decimeter rods needed to duplicate the number rod, puts them on the carrying tray, and carries them over to the first child's side of the room.

4. Together, the children assemble the decimeter rods and compare them to the target number rod, making adjustments as needed.

Extensions and Variations

- A child builds a replica of the number-rod staircase using the decimeter rods (with or without the number rods as a model).

- A child first arranges the number rods in a staircase pattern, and then uses the decimeter rods to build a set:

  - at the ends of the number rods, creating an extra-long staircase

  - as a mirror image to the number rods (that is, one staircase extends to the left, the other to the right)

  - at the ends of the number rods in inverted order (that is, 1 decimeter rod at the end of the 10-rod, 2 decimeter rods at the end of the 9-rod, and so on), resulting in a 10 x 11 rectangular arrangement

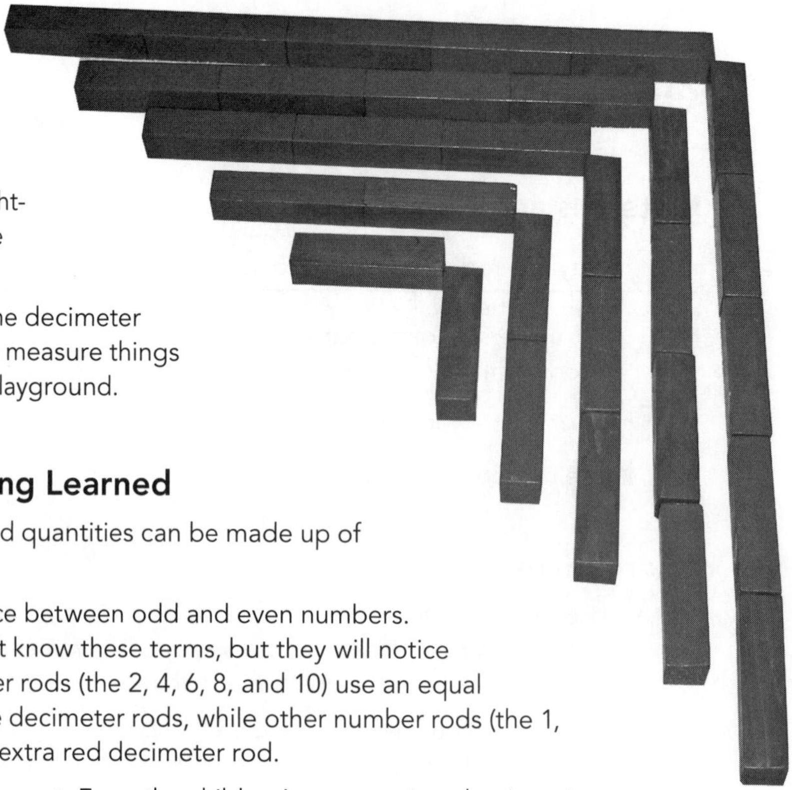

- at right
  angles to the
  corresponding
  number rods,
  forming a large, right-
  angled triangle (see
  illustration)

- Children can also use the decimeter
  rods laid end-to-end to measure things
  in the room or on the playground.

Concepts and Skills Being Learned

- Understanding that fixed quantities can be made up of
  countable sets.

- Observing the difference between odd and even numbers.
  Children probably won't know these terms, but they will notice
  that some of the number rods (the 2, 4, 6, 8, and 10) use an equal
  number of red and blue decimeter rods, while other number rods (the 1,
  3, 5, 7, and 9) require 1 extra red decimeter rod.

- Introduction to measurement. From the children's perspective, they're using
  everyday objects (called *nonstandard units of measure*) to measure things. This is
  the first developmental step in understanding measurement principles. However,
  we know they are actually using a standard metric unit of measure, the decimeter.

ADVICE COLUMN

Since children are learning new vocabulary anyway, refer to these rods by their proper
metric name. All of us in the United States need to become more comfortable using
metric units of measure, and this is a good time to start.

Ten Frames

Materials and Setup

☐ On a set of tagboard or vinyl mats, draw rectangles consisting of a 5 x 2 configuration of squares (that is, 2 rows of 5 squares each). Alternately, you can use a supply of egg cartons or ice cube trays cut to form 2 rows of 5

☐ Manipulative counters, or objects to be counted

The rule for Ten Frames is that they should always be filled from left to right and top to bottom (for example, 7 is always represented by the top row of 5 filled along with the 2 left-most squares on the bottom row—see illustration). Sticking with this routine makes every quantity from 1 to 10 recognizable by sight, without counting—a key feature that makes Ten Frames a powerful tool for developing number sense.

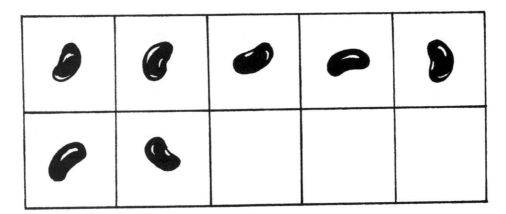

Basic Activity

1 Using a visual barrier to hide the Ten Frame from view (such as a partially opened folder, stood upright), one child puts a quantity of manipulatives inside the frame, one object per square.

2 The child briefly lifts the barrier so the other child can see, and then replaces it. The second child says how many objects she thinks are in the frame. The first child removes the barrier so the second child can verify her guess.

3 Play continues, with the children exchanging roles.

Extensions and Variations

• The Ten Frame can be used by children who are counting a collection of loose objects and wish to check their count. For example, a child who has counted a set of 8 objects can place them on the Ten Frame, see that the top row is full, as are the 3 left-most spaces on the second row, recognize this pattern, and say: "See? I was right. There are eight." More Ten Frames can be added if the count goes beyond 10.

- Similarly, the Ten Frame can be used by children as part of a more/less game to verify who has more. For example, even after one child counts her pile of objects and announces "I have eight" and another child counts his objects and says "I have six," they still may not know who has more. If they both put their objects inside the Ten Frames, they can see that the 6 objects include 1 on the bottom row, but the 8 objects include 3 on the bottom row. At this point, they can agree: "Eight is more" or "Six is less." Again, more Ten Frames can be added if the count goes beyond 10.

- Children can play "One More/One Less, Two More/Two Less." For this game, the children put the same quantity of objects on each of their Ten Frames. They then take turns saying, "We have seven in our frames. I wonder how many we would have if we had . . . one less?" The children guess out loud without moving any of their objects; then they make the change on their Ten Frames to verify the answer given. Alternatively, the caller can use a Ten Frame and a visual barrier. After showing a given quantity on the Ten Frame, she puts the barrier in place, allows the other children to see her remove or add 1 or 2 objects to the frame, and then asks the other children to predict how many are on the frame now. She then removes the barrier so the children can verify their guesses. **Note:** You can play this game with a larger group or the whole class if you use an overhead projector and a Ten Frame transparency. You can make this by photocopying a Ten Frame onto a transparency sheet or by drawing it on a plastic page protector. The caller can turn the projector on and off to show/hide the quantity inside the Ten Frame.

- Children can use playing cards showing Ten Frames with quantities 1 to 10 printed on them to play "Concentration" or "Go Fish." To play "Concentration," children need 2 cards showing 1 dot on the frame, 2 cards showing 2 dots on the frame, and so on. Children turn all cards upside down and take turns turning over two cards, trying to make matches. To play "Go Fish," children need a deck containing 4 cards of each quantity, 1 to 10. Each child is dealt 4 cards. The first child takes a turn, asking the second child, "Do you have any [name the number]s?" If the second child has any of those cards, she gives them to the first child, and the first child gets another turn. If the second child doesn't have any of the cards, she says "Go fish," and the first child draws a card from the deck. If the card drawn is the quantity the first child asked for, she gets another turn. If not, it is the second child's turn. Once a child has all 4 cards in a set, she can lay them down. Play continues till all the sets have been assembled and laid down.

- Older children can use multiple Ten Frames to divide a larger quantity into sets of 10 for easier identification of the total quantity (for example, 4 full Ten Frames and a Ten Frame with only 5 on it equals 45).

Concepts and Skills Being Learned

- Five and 10 as anchor numbers.

- Relative quantity. It's easy to visually distinguish which quantity is more when the objects are arranged in rows of 5. Four buttons don't quite fill the top row, while 6 buttons fill the top row with 1 button on the second row; therefore, 6 is greater than 4. Similarly, 12 is less than 14 because both fill 1 Ten Frame, but 12 has only 2 buttons on the second frame, while 14 has 4 on the second frame.

- Beginnings of place-value. Fourteen is seen not just as 14 discrete items but as a set of 10 plus 4 more. Twenty-two is seen as 2 sets of 10 plus 2 more. In fact, the written notations of 14 (one 10, plus 4 more) and 22 (two 10s, plus 2 more) correspond to these frames.

ADVICE COLUMN

The first step in making Ten Frames a useful tool is helping children to become familiar with the visual appearance of various quantities. They need enough practice with the frames to be able to look at the 8 and *know* that it is an 8.

Our base-10 counting system is wonderfully powerful. It has one drawback, from the young child's point of view: 10 is too big a number to visually recognize (that is, to subitize). By patterning the objects on the Ten Frame, using 5 as a base, we make the larger quantities instantly recognizable by sight.

Tabletop Rods

for ONE or MORE children

CONSTRUCTION REQUIRED

COMMERCIAL PRODUCT

Note: Tabletop rods are shorter, flatter versions of the number rods. You will need to do some construction upfront to make them. If you're not comfortable working with wood, simpler versions are described below.

Materials and Setup

☐ Tabletop rods. You can make your own set of tabletop rods by cutting ten lengths of 1 cm high x 2.5 cm wide (.4 inch x 1 inch) wood, ranging from 2.5 cm (1 inch) to 25 cm (10 inches) long. Paint each rod segment in alternating 2.5 cm (1 inch) bands of red and blue. You can also wrap the slats in alternating bands of red and blue plastic tape

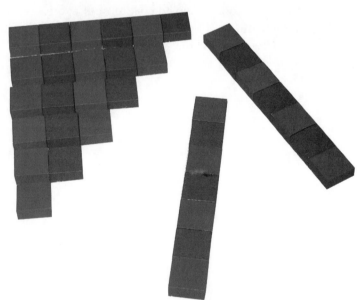

Alternatives

- Tabletop rods are also available from most Montessori suppliers. For a list of suppliers, see www.montessori.org and click on Suppliers—Montessori Materials.
- Instead of wood slats, use tagboard cut and colored according to the directions above. You will find a template for making tagboard tabletop rods on page 183.

Basic Activity

1 The child first finds the 1-rod, and then the 2-rod, and so on, counting, naming, and arranging them in stair-step fashion.

2 Play naming games with the children. Ask:
   - "Who has the _____-rod?"
   - "Where is the _____-rod?"
   - "Which one is missing?"

Extensions and Variations

- Make a different set of tabletop rods out of 1 inch wide x 1 inch long red and blue color tiles, taped together accordion-style. Using invisible tape, tape the first tile to the second across the top, tape the second to the third across the bottom, the third to the fourth across the top, alternating up to 10 (see photo). The rod can then be examined linearly and as a folded vertical stack (for example, the 8-rod folds up to create a stack of alternating red-blue tiles, 8 tiles high).

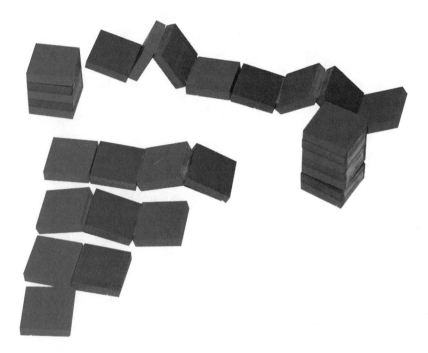

- For older children,
  - Use the tabletop rods to make larger numbers. The children can add rods to the end of the 10-rod to make higher numbers.

Concepts and Skills Being Learned

- Counting.
- Odd versus even numbers.

ADVICE COLUMN

Because tabletop rods are smaller than number rods, they are easier to use in confined spaces. See Numeral Tiles for Tabletop Rods on pages 91–92 for more activities with these materials.

The Literature Connection

COMMERCIAL
PRODUCT

ADVICE COLUMN

These books offer children practice in counting up to 10 (or down from 10). In many cases, the numeral or word name is prominently displayed on the page; usually the main focus is providing opportunities to look at and count the pictured quantities.

In many counting books, the pictured quantities are spread around a scene so that children have to count all of the objects in order to equal the specified number. This is good practice for them—they need to develop strategies for remembering which items they have already counted and which items they have yet to count.

Counting 1 to 10

Barrett, Judi. 2000. *I Knew Two Who Said Moo: A Counting and Rhyming Book*. New York: Atheneum.

Base, Graeme. 2001. *The Water Hole*. New York: Penguin.

Bassede, Francine. 1998. *George's Store at the Shore*. New York: Orchard.

Berger, Samantha. 1998. *Apples*. New York: Scholastic.

Berkes, Marianne. 2004. *Over in the Ocean: In a Coral Reef*. Nevada City, Calif.: Dawn Publications.

Bernal, Richard. 1993. *The Ants Go Marching One by One*. Lincolnwood, Ill.: Publications International.

Crews, Donald. 1968. *Ten Black Dots*. New York: Greenwillow.

Ehlert, Lois. 1990. *Fish Eyes: A Book You Can Count On*. Orlando, Fla.: Harcourt Brace.

Falwell, Cathryn. 1993. *Feast for 10*. New York: Houghton Mifflin.

Freymann, Saxton, and Joost Elffers. 2000. *One Lonely Sea Horse*. New York: Scholastic.

Gunson, Christopher. 1995. *Over on the Farm: A Counting Picture Book Rhyme*. London: Doubleday.

Kirk, David. 1994. *Miss Spider's Tea Party*. New York: Callaway Editions.

Krebs, Laurie. 2003. *We All Went on Safari: A Counting Journey through Tanzania*. Cambridge, Mass.: Barefoot Books.

Mannus, Celeste. 2002. *One Leaf Rides the Wind*. New York: Penguin.

Melmed, Laura K. 2001. *This First Thanksgiving Day: A Counting Story*. New York: HarperCollins.

Moreton, Daniel. 1998. *Animal Babies: A Counting Book*. New York: Scholastic.

Morozumi, Atsuko. 1990. *One Gorilla*. New York: Farrar, Straus and Giroux.

Parker, Kim. 2005. *Counting in the Garden*. New York: Orchard.

Parker, Vic. 1996. *Bearobics*. New York: Penguin.

Root, Phyllis. 1998. *One Duck Stuck*. Cambridge, Mass.: Candlewick.

Roth, Susan. 1997. *My Love for You*. New York: Dial.

Saul, Carol. 1998. *Barn Cat*. Boston: Little, Brown.

Schafer, Kevin. 2002. *Penguins 1 2 3*. Chanhassen, Minn.: NorthWord.

Sper, Emily. 2001. *Hanukkah: A Counting Book*. New York: Cartwheel.

Spurr, Elizabeth. 2003. *Farm Life*. New York: Holiday House.

Tafuri, Nancy. 1986. *Who's Counting?* New York: Greenwillow.

Walsh, Ellen Stoll. 1991. *Mouse Count*. Orlando, Fla.: Harcourt Brace.

Ward, Jennifer. 2002. *Over in the Garden*. Flagstaff, Ariz.: Rising Moon/ Northland.

Ziefert, Harriet. 1996. *Two Little Witches: A Halloween Counting Story*. Cambridge, Mass.: Candlewick.

Counting Backward, 10 to 1

Adams, Pam. 1979. *There Were 10 in the Bed*. Singapore: Child's Play.

Bang, Molly. 1983. *Ten, Nine, Eight*. New York: William Morrow.

Chess, Victoria. 1993. *Ten Sly Piranhas: A Counting Story in Reverse*. New York: Penguin.

Greenstein, Elaine. 2000. *Dreaming*. New York: Arthur A. Levine.

Hague, Kathleen. 1999. *Ten Little Bears: A Counting Rhyme*. New York: William Morrow.

Hutchins, Pat. 2000. *Ten Red Apples*. New York: HarperCollins.

Maccarone, Grace. 1995. *Monster Math*. New York: Scholastic.

Pallotta, Jerry. 2004. *Reese's Pieces: Count by Tens*. New York: Scholastic.

Sheppard, Jeff. 1990. *The Right Number of Elephants*. New York: HarperCollins.

Singer, Marilyn. 2002. *Quiet Night*. New York: Clarion.

Stockham, Jess. 2003. *Ten Little Speckled Frogs*. Singapore: Child's Play.

Wood, Audrey. 2004. *Ten Little Fish*. New York: Blue Sky.

4

recognizing and writing numerals 0 to 9

Adults who work with children don't often distinguish between practicing numbers and practicing numerals. Children can develop a solid understanding of quantities without ever understanding what the numerical symbols *3* and *8* mean. They also can be confused by the difference between the symbols *6* and *9,* and *13* and *31,* even when they are not confused about the number of objects before them.

The activities in chapter 4 build on children's ability to count quantities by providing lots of practice in recognizing the written symbols for numbers. They also help children develop the physical skills necessary for writing numerals correctly. Children should be working on the activities in this chapter if

- they aren't sure what to call a numeral when they're shown it

- they're uncertain how to form a numeral, tend to write some of their numerals backward, or use an incorrect series of strokes to form numerals

Sandpaper or Felt Numerals

Materials and Setup

You can purchase commercial sets of sandpaper numerals from most Montessori distributors, or you can make your own set according to the instructions below.

☐ Ten sturdy wood boards measuring 11 cm x 14 cm (approximately 4 ¼ inches x 5 ½ inches). This is the size of half a letter-sized page. Tagboard also works, but it isn't as durable

☐ Large-sized numerals 0 to 9 cut out of sandpaper or felt (see page 185 for a template)

☐ Colored dot stickers

☐ Mystery bag (optional) (see page 27 for more information)

☐ Manipulatives or counters in a basket (optional)

Glue the sandpaper or felt numerals onto the boards. Attach a colored dot sticker to each of the numerals at the starting point of the strokes needed to trace/draw the numeral. With a permanent marker, draw numerals on the dots to indicate the order of the strokes, and then draw short arrows extending from the dots to indicate the direction of the strokes.

Design Note: If you're making your own sandpaper or felt numerals, use sans serif numerals (ones that do not include curls or straight lines at the end of strokes). For 4s and 9s, use a straight-line style such as the one shown to the right: In other words, the strokes making up the numerals should be exactly the same as the hand motions you want the child to practice in forming them.

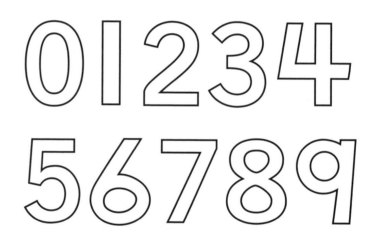

Some educators are moving toward use of italicized or D'Nealian printing, believing that doing so helps children make the transition to cursive writing more easily, but I believe straight-line letters and numerals are still the best starting point for young hands.

Basic Activity

1 Children trace a numeral with 2 fingers (the extended middle and pointer fingers of their dominant hands), saying the name of the numeral as they trace it.

Extensions and Variations

- As you play this game, adjust your verbal prompts to children's current level of number-name awareness:

  - Level One: "This is the one . . . this is the two . . . this is the three." Here, you are providing the label for the child.

  - Level Two: "Who has the two?" "Bring me the two." "Which one is the two?" "Show me how to write the two." Here, children should point to the correct numeral. They need to recognize the name and know what it means (known as *receptive language*) but do not have to say the name themselves (known as *expressive language*). If they hesitate or make errors at this level, return to the first level.

  - Level Three: "Which one is this?" "What numerals did you turn over?" "Which numeral is missing?" "What numeral do you feel in the bag?" "What numeral did you just write?" Here children must come up with the name themselves. This is the hardest of the three levels. If they are struggling with this, return to the second or first level.

- Place the sandpaper numerals in a mystery bag. Children reach into the bag, trace the numeral they feel, and select from a basket the number of objects that correspond to the numeral. They then remove the numeral from the bag and place it with the objects.

- Children bring an appropriate number of objects from various parts of the room to place on their sandpaper numerals. For example, they might bring 6 crayons from the art area or 6 toy cars from the block area and place them on the 6 numeral. They return all objects when they are done.

Concepts and Skills Being Learned

- Names of numerals.
- Visual recognition of numerals.
- Muscle memory for how to write numerals.

ADVICE COLUMN

Young children do not need to practice writing numerals (or letters) on lined paper. However, it is important for them to develop the muscle sense for properly forming the numerals. When the large muscles of their arms develop the habit making the right sequence of motions to form a numeral, the small muscles of their hands and wrists naturally follow.

For these reasons, insist that children follow the guidelines of the coding dots and arrows rather than coming up with their own way of tracing the numerals. Now is the time to develop good habits (however, note the addendum to this advice in the Advice Column for the next activity on page 73).

As you have probably noticed, I consistently use the word *numeral* rather than *number* when referring to the written symbol, not the quantity. It is important when talking with fellow educators to make this distinction. However, it is not necessary when talking with children. It's much more natural to say to them, "What number is this?" than "What numeral is this?" and it does them no harm.

Cornmeal Tray Numeral Tracing

for **ONE** or **MORE** children

Materials and Setup

☐ Cooking tray, cake pan, or similar flat-bottomed container with a rim

☐ Cornmeal, salt, sand, or a similar substance

☐ Sandpaper numerals 0 to 9 (see pages 70–71)

Pour enough cornmeal, salt, or sand into the cooking tray to barely cover its bottom.

Basic Activity

1 The child practices tracing a sandpaper numeral and saying its name.

2 The child then traces the same numeral in the bottom of the cornmeal tray, using the extended middle and pointer fingers of the dominant hand, and says the numeral's name.

3 The child gently shakes the tray to erase the numeral and repeats the sequence with a different numeral.

Extensions and Variations

• Instead of cornmeal, use fingerpaint or shaving cream on a protected tabletop.

• One child traces a numeral on a second child's back. The second child points to the sandpaper numeral he thinks matches the numeral traced on his back. The first child verifies that this is correct, or retraces the numeral for the second child to guess again.

• Let the children use the overhead projector to project a sandpaper numeral onto a wall. Post a large piece of paper on the wall and have the children practice tracing the numeral within the outlined image. If the image is projected onto a chalkboard or whiteboard, the children can use chalk or wipe-off markers to write the numerals.

• Provide chalk sticks for the children to use to make gigantic numerals on the classroom chalkboard or the sidewalk outdoors.

Concept and Skill Being Learned

• Recognizing, naming, and writing numerals.

ADVICE COLUMN

It is useful to have children trace the numeral shape with the pointer finger and middle finger rather than with the pointer finger alone. When it comes time to add a writing implement, it's a simple matter of adding the thumb to create the classic three-finger grasp. **Note:** There is a similar rationale for adding knobs to the various puzzles in the room: by having children manipulate the puzzle pieces by grasping a knob, you are helping them strengthen the pincer grasp used for writing.

As mentioned in the last activity, it is important to make sure that children trace the sandpaper numerals using the correct sequence of movements. Don't correct them when they make their own numerals freehand, however. They are attempting to remember what they have learned on the sandpaper numeral, and they will continue to make errors for a while. Let the materials provide the correction. Keep playing naming and tracing games with the sandpaper numerals until the proper motor sequence becomes habitual.

Rainbow Numeral Tracing

Materials and Setup

☐ Photocopies of the numerals for the numeral relay (see pages 186–195). Outline the photocopied numbers in black, and include coding arrows with the starting points for tracing strokes marked and numbered

☐ An assortment of colored markers, pencils, or crayons in a rainbow of colors

Design Note: An interesting variation that saves paper makes use of translucent, wipe-off posterboard, which is inexpensive and available at many craft stores. Mount a half page (5.5 inch x 8 inch) sheet of the wipe-off posterboard onto tagboard or stiff cardboard by taping it along 3 of its edges. Leave 1 side open, so the photocopied page can be slipped between the posterboard and the tagboard (see photo). The numeral's outline remains visible through the translucent material. The child can write on the wipe-off material with a dry-erase marker and then erase, instead of writing on the paper itself.

Basic Activity

1 Children use one of the writing implements and write the numeral once on the sheet, using the appropriate series of strokes.

2 They choose a second writing implement of a different color and on the same piece of paper write the numeral again, within the outline.

3 They continue until they have used all the writing implements to trace the numeral. The result is a numeral that has been traced in a rainbow of colors.

4 They can then select another sheet of the same or a different numeral and repeat the activity.

Concept and Skill Being Learned

- Recognizing, naming, and writing numerals.

ADVICE COLUMN

This is a better way for young hands to practice forming their numerals than the traditional method of tracing dotted numerals for several reasons:

1. The numeral writing is practiced on a much larger scale, relying more on large-motor than fine-motor control. The emphasis is less on the fingers controlling the writing instrument and more on the hand moving in a patterned sequence of steps through space.

2. Children still have to make their own path within the broad outline instead of following a narrow path of dots already drawn for them.

3. Children focus upon the sweeping motion of their strokes rather than on moving from dot to dot.

Telephone Dialing

for **ONE** or **MORE** children

Materials and Setup

☐ One or two touch-tone or rotary telephones

☐ A Rolodex or list containing the children's first names and telephone numbers
Note: Include only phone numbers for children whose parents have given permission.

Basic Activity

1 A child looks up the name of the child he wishes to call in the Rolodex or on the phone list located in the dramatic play area.

2 The child dials the number on the telephone and carries on conversation with the imaginary person who answers.

Extensions and Variations

Provide a second role-playing phone so the child whose number is dialed can answer and make the call a two-way conversation.

Concepts and Skills Being Learned

• Matching numerals in the Rolodex or on the list to those on the phone.

• Finding numerals in sequential (rotary) and patterned (touch-tone) arrangements.

ADVICE COLUMN

A wide variety of numerals in children's environments don't actually represent quantities. Phone numbers are a case in point. Home addresses and sports players' jerseys are other examples. These numerals nonetheless afford opportunities for the child to practice recognizing and naming numerals.

Numeral Relay

Materials and Setup

☐ Two sets of large numerals 1 to 9 cut out of tagboard. See pages 186–195 for templates

☐ Two lines on the ground, approximately 20 meters (20 yards) apart; masking tape, ropes, or traffic cones work well

☐ Two mystery bags large enough to contain the numerals (optional)

Basic Activity

This activity can be played outdoors or indoors.

1. Children divide themselves into 2 teams.

2. The 2 teams line up behind the starting line. Behind the other line are the 2 sets of numerals in random order.

3. At the "Go" signal, the first child in each line races to the other end of the course, finds the numeral 1, brings it back to the starting line, and lays the numeral on the ground.

4. The race continues with the next child in each line racing to the other end, finding the next numeral, bringing it back to the starting line, and placing it to the right of the numerals already retrieved. When the children have cycled through the line, the first child goes again, until all of the numbers have been retrieved.

5. The game ends when both teams have all of their numerals.

Extensions and Variations

- Children can all belong to a single team and simply take turns retrieving the next numeral.

- They can retrieve the numerals in reverse order (that is, starting with 9). Numeral 0 can be in added to the set, and possibly 10. When a team retrieves the 0, the children can yell "Blast-off!"

- Place each set of numerals in a separate mystery bag. Team members must find the numeral by feel rather than by sight.

Concepts and Skills Being Learned

- Numeral recognition.
- Numerical order.
- Counting forward and backward.

ADVICE COLUMN

Make sure all children have a chance to participate and be successful. For example, if one of them needs assistance recognizing numerals, he can ask another child to accompany him and help him locate the appropriate numeral, but he should bring the numeral back himself. If a child has a physical disability, she can line up close to the numeral end and work with a designated runner. When her runner arrives, she can hand him the numeral she has chosen and have him take it back to the starting line.

Wikki Stix, Playdough, and Bodies

for **ONE** or **MORE** children

COMMERCIAL PRODUCT

Materials and Setup

☐ Anything bendable or moldable, such as playdough, Wikki Stix (available from many educational suppliers), pipe cleaners, or yarn

☐ Numeral cards (optional) (see page 13)

Basic Activity

1 The child forms the designated material into the shape of various numerals.

Extensions and Variations

- Children draw a card from the numeral deck to decide what numeral to make next.
- They arrange the numerals they've created in numerical order.
- A group of children arrange their bodies on the floor to form a specific numeral.
- Provide a length of rope or yarn. A group of children pick up the rope and hold it at waist level, positioning themselves and their hands to shape the rope into a specific numeral.

Concept and Skill Being Learned

- Visual recognition of numerals.

ADVICE COLUMN

These are fun activities, but recognize them for what they are. Molding material into the shape of a numeral does not help children develop the muscle sense for writing numerals. It does, however, strengthen their sense of what numerals look like and gives them added practice at recognizing and naming numerals.

Numeral Sorting

for **ONE** or **MORE** children

Materials and Setup

☐ A container, such as a shoe box or a plastic bin

☐ Cut-outs of numerals 0 to 9 in a variety of sizes and fonts. You can cut these from various magazines or make them on your computer. Mount the numerals on tagboard or cardboard so they are easier to manipulate

☐ Key cards, 0 to 9, to designate categories (see page 13)

Basic Activity

1 Children arrange the key cards in sequence.

2 They then sort the numerals into their appropriate categories.

Extensions and Variations

Children explore typing numerals in various sizes and fonts on the computer.

Concepts and Skills Being Learned

- Numeral recognition.
- Classification.

ADVICE COLUMN

Numeral recognition is commonly treated as if it were a simple matter of identifying 10 symbols. In fact, a particular numeral can be written many ways. Consider, for example, the following numerals.

Each 4 is very different in appearance, yet all represent the quantity 4.

Golf

Materials and Setup

☐ Discs (colored plastic plates, or cardboard circles sealed in contact paper) to serve as targets or holes

☐ Flags numbered 0 to 9, to be placed near the discs; you can make these using straws or wooden dowels and laminated construction paper

☐ Outdoor play equipment: a plastic golf set, beanbags, croquet set, or Frisbees all work well

Basic Activity

This activity can be done outdoors or indoors in a large open space.

1 Have children arrange the discs and numbered flags on the ground in any configuration they choose.

2 Starting at the 0 flag, children putt a golf ball, throw a beanbag, toss a Frisbee, or hit a croquet ball from one disc to the next in numerical order. The shot must touch the disc to count as being in the hole.

Extensions and Variations

Provide the child with pages from any commercial connect-the-dots workbook. The child starts at 1 and connects the dots to reveal the hidden picture. You can create more durable materials by laminating the pages and providing the children with a wipe-off marker.

Concepts and Skills Being Learned

• Numeral recognition.

• Numerical order.

ADVICE COLUMN

Trust children to adjust the difficulty of the task in terms of physical distance and the order of the holes. They will make their game easier while they remain uncertain, and harder once they gain confidence.

Path Card Numerals

Materials and Setup

☐ Set of path cards with path segments printed on them that connect when the cut pieces are laid side by side (See page 196–205 for templates.)

☐ Display cards showing numerals constructed from path cards. Display cards are simply smaller versions of path cards that haven't been cut into pieces

Basic Activity

1 Children select and arrange path cards to make the target numeral shown on the display card.

Extensions and Variations

- An easier version: Make the display cards the same size as the numeral made from the path cards (with or without the card outlines showing). Children can place the path cards directly on the display card to construct the numeral.

- A harder version: Children construct the numeral free-form.

Concepts and Skills Being Learned

- Numeral recognition.

- Shapes and directions that make up numerals.

ADVICE COLUMN

As you might suspect, path cards are designed mainly for exploring geometry. However, this variation allows them to explore numerals.

Classroom Signs

Materials and Setup

☐ Signs with numerals on them, posted in the classroom for various purposes (for example, to control how many children are in an area or to show how many snack items to take)

Basic Activity

1 As often as possible, post meaningful signs throughout the classroom that include numerals. Children learn to read the signs and either do what they say or learn something about the classroom's environment.

Extensions and Variations

- Include rebus recipe cards in your classroom. You can buy these commercially or make your own. For example, instead of writing the term *3 cups,* write a *3* with a picture of a cup after it. At the snack table, display a *3* with a cracker drawn after it to show the children that they should serve themselves three crackers.

- Place a set of command cards on the shelf—2 decks of cards, 1 of which shows actions, such as jumping, skipping, or rolling, and the other a deck of numeral cards. The child draws a card from each deck and performs the pictured action the indicated number of times. You can make command cards using clip art or, for added interest, you can use photos of the children as the models for the picture set. For example, cards can show different children from your room jumping high in the air, rolling on the floor, hopping on one foot, throwing a ball in the air, or putting on a coat.

Concept and Skill Being Learned

- Numbers are used in everyday life.

ADVICE COLUMN

Use picture icons as well as numerals in your classroom postings so even those children who don't know their numerals can read the signs. If children are generally aware of a rule (for example, how many of them are allowed in the reading area at one time), you can eliminate the pictured quantities so they have only the numerals as reminders. Children connect their knowledge of how many are allowed in the area with the sight of the numeral. And if someone occasionally makes a mistake, you can be sure a friend will point it out.

The Literature Connection

COMMERCIAL
PRODUCT

ADVICE COLUMN

The following books explore the shapes of numerals and their matching number names. Children enjoy trying to find numerals that are embedded in pictures; these are often cleverly camouflaged as parts of everyday objects in these books.

Numerals to 10

Canizares, Susan. 1999. *Numbers All Around*. New York: Scholastic.

Keller, Laurie. 2005. *Grandpa Gazillion's Number Yard*. New York: Henry Holt.

Liebler, John. 1994. *Frog Counts to Ten*. Brookfield, Conn.: Millbrook.

MacDonald, Suse. 1988. *Numblers*. New York: Scholastic.

————. 1989. *Puzzlers*. New York: Penguin.

————. 2000. *Look Whooo's Counting*. New York: Scholastic.

Martin, Bill, Jr. 2001. *Rock It, Sock It, Number Line*. New York: Henry Holt.

Numerals to 100

Martin, Bill, Jr., Michael Sampson, and Lois Ehlert. 2004. *Chicka Chicka 1-2-3*. New York: Simon & Schuster.

5

connecting numerals to quantities

In my Montessori training, I learned that first comes the concrete, then the abstract, and then the connection between the concrete and the abstract. This is certainly true when it come to number sense. Once children know how to count accurately and have a stable sense of quantity (the concrete), we teach them numerals (the abstract). We then teach them to match the quantity with the numeral (connecting the concrete to the abstract). In chapter 5, you will find activities that help children exercise this last connection. Generally, those who have a stable sense of quantity, know how to count, and know their numerals make the transition easily to matching quantities to numerals.

Pencil Boxes

Materials and Setup

 Pencil boxes 1 to 10 (see below for instructions on how to construct them)

Fifty-five unsharpened pencils, in a basket

Constructing the Pencil Boxes

Here are descriptions of two different ways to create the pencil boxes. The first is more labor intensive, but it's also more customizable. The second can be made from materials available at most office supply stores, but isn't an exact fit. The pencil boxes are a variation on a standard piece of Montessori equipment called *spindle boxes*. To check out what spindle boxes look like and how much they cost, check out the list of suppliers on the Montessori Foundation's Web site at www.montessori.org.

Version I

1 Create two boxes out of wood or heavy cardboard (see illustration below). Each box will be 21.5 cm wide x 20 cm deep x 2 cm high (8.5 inches x 8 inches x ¾ inch). However, the back wall will be slightly higher, at 5.5 cm (2.25 inches), and the front wall will be made of clear stiff plastic (you might recycle a piece of plastic packaging that merchandise often comes sealed in).

2 Add dividers to each box, so that each box is divided into 5 side-by-side compartments 4 cm wide x 20 cm deep x 2 cm high (1.5 inches x 8 inches x ¾ inch).

3 On the back wall of the first box, write the numerals 1 through 5 so that one numeral appears above each compartment. In the same manner, write the numerals 6 through 10 in the second box. The numerals should be written in green, except for the tens digit in the 10-compartment, which should be written in blue.

4 On the clear plastic front wall of the boxes, use a green permanent marker to draw two rows of five squares (like a small Ten Frame—see pages 61–63) in front of each compartment. Then outline each Ten Frame with a blue permanent marker.

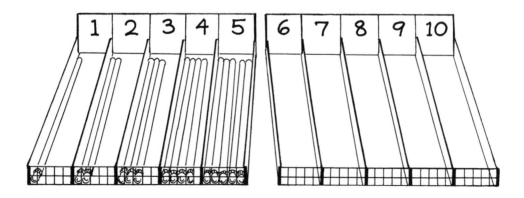

Version II

Instead of building the wooden boxes, you could use a plastic 3-drawer storage container found in many office supply stores. Each drawer of the container is only wide enough for 4 compartments, but it works quite well to divide the top drawer into the 1- through 4-compartments, the second drawer into the 5- through 8-compartments, and the third drawer into the 9- and 10-compartments (see photo). Use cardboard or tagboard taped to the bottoms and sides of each drawer as the dividers. It's not a perfect fit, but it's easier to construct than Version I.

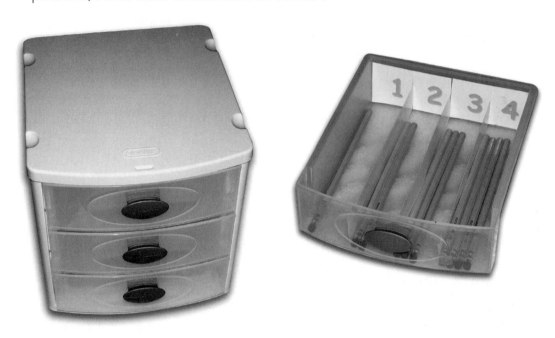

Basic Activity

1. Children pick up 1 pencil from the basket and place it in the 1-compartment.

2. They continue to pick up pencils one at a time with their dominant hand, count them into their other hand ("One . . . two"), and place them in the next compartment. They continue this activity, placing 2 pencils in the 2-compartment, and so on, until all the compartments have been filled.

   Note: This activity works best when children keep all of the pencils' erasers pointing toward the front of the compartment so that they can be seen through the front. The pencils' erasers look like dots filling up a Ten Frame.

Extensions and Variations

- When filling compartments 6 through 10, children can insert a cardboard rectangle to separate the bottom layer (that is, the first 5 pencils) from the top layer. This emphasizes the numeral 5 as an anchor number and makes the similarity between the first 5 compartments and the second 5 compartments more striking (for example, the 2-compartment has 2 pencils in it, and the 7-compartment has 2 pencils sitting on top of the cardboard).

- With children's permission, remove the sets of pencils from the compartments and place the sets in random order in front of them (or, as a greater challenge, on a table across the room). Then, point to one of the sets and ask, "Which compartment do these go in?" or point to a compartment and ask, "Which pencils belong in here?"

Concepts and Skills Being Learned

- Recognizing numerals.

- Associating quantities with numerals.

- Five as an anchor number (for example, 7 is 5 plus 2 more).

ADVICE COLUMN

On one level, this is a simple activity that involves accurately counting and matching quantities with numerals. On another level, it prepares children to appreciate numbers in a whole new way—as part of a hierarchical system of place values.

This is a good place to pause and appreciate the implications of this educational approach. If we give children well-designed materials and let them explore mathematical relationships at their own pace, we don't actually need to teach them complex concepts, such as place value. In fact, Piaget would caution us that children of this age *can't* be taught these concepts.

Instead, what we're doing is giving them a chance to gradually discover these relationships for themselves, through their own thoughts and activity. Children with access to these materials grapple with these concepts on their own timetable and construct their understandings slowly, through personally meaningful attempts to understand their own experiences. Providing information in this way constitutes truly child-centered education, or what I like to call *hands-on, minds-on learning*. When these principles are pointed out to children more explicitly some years down the line, they simply accept the new words used to describe relationships they already understand at a visceral level.

Unifix Stairs

Materials and Setup

☐ Tray for holding Unifix stacks, 1 to 10 blocks long, in stair-step fashion.
This is a commercial product often called a Unifix stair that can be found at most educational supply outlets, including Lakeshore, www.lakeshorelearning.com; Didax, www.didax.com; and Discount School Supply, www.discountschoolsupply.com

☐ 55 Unifix cubes in 10 different colors. (Make sure you have enough of each color to make 10 color-coded stacks. A different color is needed for each of the stacks, 1 to 10.)

Alternatives

Many classrooms have a variety of teacher-made and commercial materials that provide physical feedback on assigning correct quantity to numerals (for example, nested stacking cubes with printed numerals and quantities on them; wooden bead-stackers; quantity/numeral puzzle sets, all numbered 1 to 10).

Basic Activity

1 Children sort the cubes by color.

2 They snap a color set together, counting each cube as it is added.

3 They look at the numerals on the tray and decide in which compartment to put that color stack.

Extensions and Variations

- Children assemble the Unifix stacks and put them in a stair-step arrangement outside the tray.

- With their permission, remove the stacks from the tray, put them in front of the children in random order, point to a numeral on the tray, and ask, "Which stack goes in this compartment?"

- Children count the stacks backward (for example, "This is five, see? Five, four, three, two, one . . . zero.").

- Add a 1-to-10 numeral card deck to the set. The children divide the Unifix stacks equally among themselves (they can hide them behind their backs if they wish). They then turn over the numeral cards one at a time and ask, "Who has the _____?" The child who thinks she has that quantity reveals her stack, sets it next to the card, and points to the cubes one at a time while the group counts aloud.

- Children play a more/less game by dividing up the Unifix stacks among themselves and taking turns asking more/less questions (for example, "I have 7. Who has a stack that is 2 less than mine?") Children set their Unifix stacks side-by-side to verify their answers.

Concepts and Skills Being Learned

- Cardinality principle.
- Numeral recognition.
- Associating quantities with numerals.
- Numerical order.

ADVICE COLUMN

This is one of those activities with excellent built-in control of error. Let's say a child has just counted the green Unifix stack and decides it is a 5-stack:

- If she miscounted, she either finds the 5-compartment already occupied or sees that the green Unifix stack doesn't fit when she tries to place it in the 5-compartment.

- If she counted accurately but doesn't know what the 5 looks like, she can keep trying different compartments until she finds the one that fits, thereby discovering what the numeral for 5 looks like.

Whichever of these is true, she doesn't need an adult to check her work for accuracy. Her work is self-correcting.

This is both the strength and the weakness of activities with built-in control of error. Notice that this child could, in fact, complete the activity successfully without knowing what she was doing or paying attention to the quantities or the numerals. If you want to make certain a child is practicing a specific skill, you need to ensure that he also engages in other activities that don't control for error. These types of activities are good for helping children to build their skills slowly in a success-oriented environment.

Numeral Tiles for Tabletop Rods

Materials and Setup

☐ 30 red and 25 blue tiles, 2.5 cm square (1 inch x 1 inch). You can buy a commercial set of wooden tiles from most educational suppliers, or you can make your own from colored tagboard. Using a green permanent marker, label the tiles according to these specifications:

☐ Red tiles: 10 tiles with numeral 1; 8 tiles with the numeral 3; 6 tiles with the numeral 5; 4 with the numeral 7; 2 with the numeral 9

☐ Blue tiles: 9 with numeral 2; 7 with numeral 4; 5 with numeral 6; 3 with numeral 8; 1 with numeral 10. On the 10-tile, write the 10s digit in blue, and the 1s digit in green

☐ Tabletop rods (see pages 64–65)

Basic Activity

1 Children sort the tiles according to numeral.

2 Starting with the 1-rod, they count the sections and place the tiles, selecting the appropriate numeral to put on top of each rod segment as they go. (For example, when doing the 3-rod, they say "One," find the 1-tile, and place it on the first segment of the rod; say "Two," find the 2-tile, and place it on the second segment of the rod; say "Three," find the 3-tile, and place it on the last segment of the rod.) See photo.

3 Once the numeral tiles are all placed, children point to and count the numeral sequence on the rod (for example, "One, two, three.").

Extensions and Variations

- Children stack the numerals tiles vertically next to the tabletop rods, creating stacks of tiles in increasing height (for example, the stack next to the 5-rod would have a 1-tile on the bottom, a 2-tile on top of that, and then a 3-tile, a 4-tile, and a 5-tile). Note that the stack always has the numeral naming the rod on top of it (for example, the 8-rod stack of tiles has the numeral 8 showing on top of a stack 8 tiles tall).

- Children lay the numeral tiles horizontally at the end of the corresponding rod (for example, they put the 6 tiles with the numeral 5 on them at the end of the 5-rod). This creates a 10 x 11 configuration of rods and tiles.

- Children practice counting backward through the stacked tile sequences (for example, they take apart the stack next to the 5-rod, naming the numerals as they are exposed: "Five, four, three, two, one.").

- For children who do not know their numerals up to 10, provide only the rods 1 to 5 and their accompanying tiles.

Concepts and Skills Being Learned

- Recognizing numerals.

- Placing numerals in correct sequential order.

- Associating the oral counting sequence ("One, two, three, four . . .") with the numeral counting sequence (1, 2, 3, 4 . . .).

- The cardinality principle.

- Counting backward.

- Children may discover many other number-numeral patterns. For example, the row of numerals on top of the 5-rod is identical to that covering the 4-rod, except the numeral 5 is added.

- It takes 5 tiles to count up to the numeral 5.

- When children lift parts of the stacked tiles for the 8-rod, they see the numeral telling them how tall the remaining stack is (for example, when they remove 3 tiles from the 8-rod stack, they see the numeral 5, which indicates that the stack is now 5 tiles high).

ADVICE COLUMN

You've probably noticed that the colors of the tiles correspond to the colors of the sections of the tabletop rods. This feature helps children observe the alternating odd-even numbers. The colors of the numerals foreshadow another design element: they draw attention to the place value of the numbers, with units being colored green and 10s blue.

These small design features may not seem like much yet, but they become increasingly important as children progress through the activities in this book and in materials later in the math sequence. Consistency in the design of materials helps children understand the underlying concepts.

Plates and Clothespins

Materials and Setup

☐ 10 sturdy picnic plates, paper or plastic

☐ Colored dot stickers. Place between 1 and 10 dots on the plates, equally spaced around the rim. Use one plate for each quantity, 1 to 10

☐ Numeral cards, 1 to 10 (see page 13)

☐ 55 spring clothespins with numerals 1 to 10 written on them in permanent ink. There should be ten 1s, nine 2s, eight 3s, and so on

Basic Activity

1 Children pick a plate and count the dots.

2 They then attach clothespins to the coding dots, starting with the 1-clothespin and proceeding in numerical order around the plate.

3 They then place the appropriate numeral card on the plate.

Extensions and Variations

• Children use the plates as trays for sorting the clothespins, putting all of the 5-clothespins on the plate with 5 dots, and so on.

• Once the clothespins have been attached, the plates can be used for a guessing game. One child places a plate under a blanket. Another child reaches under the blanket, names the plate by feeling the number of clothespins around the rim, and pulls the plate out to verify his guess.

• To expose children to the written names of the numbers, label the center of the plates with the number name (for example, write the word *five* on the plate that has 5 dots).

• For children who do not yet recognize numerals, use plates that have the coding dots for sequential numerals already written on them. The child counts each dot out loud, finds a clothespin with a matching numeral, and attaches it to the dot.

Concepts and Skills Being Learned

• Counting numerals in sequential order.

• Associating numerals with quantities.

• The cardinality principle: in this case, the last clothespin attached names the number of clothespins on the plate.

ADVICE COLUMN

The time spent finding and manipulating the clothespins in sequence forces children to re-establish the counting sequence each time (for example, "Okay, that was the three. Which one do I need next? One, two, three . . . four."). Over time, they no longer have to start over again at 1 to confidently pick up the count (for example, "Okay, that was the three. What's next? Three . . . four.").

This is also a good activity for helping children develop the fine-motor control and pincer strength that are needed for writing.

Picture-Sorting Sets

Materials and Setup

☐ Pictures showing various objects in sets of 1 to 10. You can take digital pictures of sets, cut suitable pictures from magazines, or make sets using construction paper and clip art or stickers. There should be at least 4 to 5 picture sets for each quantity

☐ Key cards showing numerals 1 to 10 (see page 13)

Basic Activity

1 Children set out the key cards in numerical order, left to right.

2 They sort the pictures by quantity.

Extensions and Variations

- Include several picture cards that are blank, and add a numeral card labeled 0.
- Children can use the picture sets to play Showdown (see pages 40–41) or Number-Numeral Concentration (see pages 98–99).

Concepts and Skills Being Learned

- Associating quantities with numerals.
- Classifying objects according to quantity: pictures showing three marbles and three umbrellas belong together, but pictures showing three marbles and six marbles do not.

ADVICE COLUMN

One way to give children more ownership of activities like this one is to use a digital camera. Let the children assemble sets of objects (for example, 3 dolls, 6 hairbands, 5 race cars, 2 clay sculptures, etc.), take pictures of those sets, print them, and add the pictures to the sorting activity. If their own faces are included in the pictures of the sets they created, the appeal is even greater.

More-Less-Same Sorting II

Materials and Setup

☐ 20 to 30 bowls or plates, each holding between 1 and 10 objects (for example, Unifix cubes, beads, toy cars, etc.)

☐ Numeral cards, 2 to 9 (see page 13)

☐ More, less, and same labels (see page 179). You can add the symbols <, =, and > if you wish

Basic Activity

1 Children set out the labels *less*, *same*, and *more*, left to right.

2 They choose a numeral card and set it above the *same* label. This is the target numeral for them to use in determining more, less, or the same.

3 They place the bowls of objects under the appropriate labels. For example, if the target numeral is 5, they place the bowls with 5 objects under the *same* label, bowls with fewer than 5 objects under the *less* label, and bowls with more than 5 objects under the *more* label.

Extensions and Variations

One child selects a secret number from the pile of numeral cards. Other children take turns verbally guessing what that number might be. After each guess, the first child picks up either the *more* label or the *less* label to indicate whether the next child should choose a larger or smaller number. When a child guesses the correct number, the first child holds up the *same* label and shows the target numeral card. **Note:** This game is very challenging for young children. Figuring out whether one number is greater than another without having a set of objects to use as a reference is an advanced skill.

Concepts and Skills Being Learned

• Relative quantity, this time lumping multiple quantities into the same category of *more* or *less*.

• Understanding the terms *less*, *same*, and *more*.

ADVICE COLUMN

Children become more invested in this activity when they have a hand in creating the manipulative sets for sorting. Have them gather materials to put in the sorting bowls. This takes longer, but efficiency isn't everything. Remember: most of these activities will be stored on a shelf for children to pull out any time. As a teacher, you need to develop routines that allow children to perform activities without your help or supervision.

There's some debate about the proper vocabulary to use for activities such as this. Should you say "more," "more than," or "greater than"? As best I can tell, when you're comparing one set of objects to another set (for example, two bowls of fruit), you should say, "This bowl has more than that one" or "This bowl has more." If you're comparing numbers in the abstract, with no reference to objects (for example, the numeral 6 and the numeral 3), you should say, "Six is greater than 3." Is this a big deal? Not to me, and certainly not to children. In the long run, they need to become familiar with all the different ways of referring to quantities, so don't worry too much about what term to use on different occasions.

Number-Numeral Concentration

Materials and Setup

☐ Numeral cards, 0 to 10 (see page 13)

☐ Picture cards, 0 to 10 (see page 13)

Basic Activity

1 Children lay all 20 cards (10 showing quantities, 10 showing numerals) face down, in random positions.

2 They take turns flipping over 2 cards. If the pictured quantity and the numeral match, the child keeps the trick. If they do not match, the child flips the 2 cards back over and the next child takes a turn (see also Quantity Concentration on pages 21–22).

Extensions and Variations

- Use fewer cards if children become frustrated trying to make matches with so many cards to choose from or if they are uncomfortable with quantities and numerals up to 10. You might try limiting quantities and numerals to 5 or less.

- If the children are unsure of their numerals, you can draw small counting dots on the numeral cards. When you do so, you create a bridge set between Quantity Concentration (pages 21–22) and the Number-Numeral Concentration game described here. Each time children flip over a numeral card, they can count the dots, if necessary, to remind themselves what the name of the numeral is. You need to observe carefully to determine how much children are relying on the coding dots versus the numerals to make the match. If they are that shaky about numerals, you may want to go back to some of the activities outlined in chapter 3.

Concept and Skill Being Learned

- Mentally representing quantities and numerals together so that one reminds the child of the other.

ADVICE COLUMN

One of the best pieces of advice I ever received regarding young children and number sense goes like this: "We need to keep treating numbers as adjectives as long as possible rather than using them as nouns." What does that mean? Young children's sense of quantity is grounded in the concrete world. They can deal with 9 crayons much easier than they can deal with the word *nine* or the numeral 9. In the first case, 9 describes the crayons (in other words, it functions as an adjective). In the second case, 9 is an entity in its own right (that is, it functions as a noun). The Number-Numeral Concentration activity described here, and other activities like it, form a bridge between these concepts. One card shows the number as an adjective (that is, as a quantity of objects), while the other card shows the number as a noun (in other words, as a numeral). To make the match from memory, children need to find a common language to represent the two in their minds.

Number-Numeral Bingo

for **THREE** or more children

Materials and Setup, Format A

- Numeral cards, 0 to 10 (see page 13)

- Bingo cards in a 4 x 4 or 5 x 5 configuration. A blank template for these cards appears on page 206; you can laminate copies of the cards or glue each card to a piece of tagboard. On each square on the grid, draw 0 to 10 icons, or use small stickers. (Multiple squares on the card should have the same quantity.) Depending on how many children you have in your group, make a variety of cards, each with a different arrangement of the icons in the squares; this way, the children can't all win at the same time

- Lima beans or other manipulatives to cover the squares as they get called

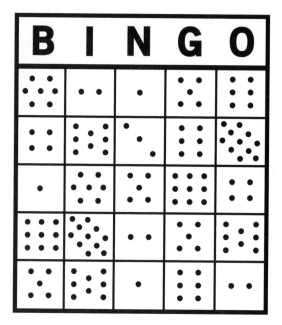

Materials and Setup, Format B

- Picture cards, 0 to 10 (see page 13)

- Bingo cards made from tagboard or laminated paper in a 4 x 4 or 5 x 5 configuration. See page 206 for a template. Each square on the grid should show a numeral, 0 to 10 (multiple squares on the card can have the same numeral)

- Lima beans or other manipulatives to cover the squares as they get called

Note: Format A is slightly harder for young children because they have to scan and count multiple sets of objects on the Bingo card, looking for ones that might be the same quantity as the numeral shown on the calling card. In Format B, children only have to count one set of objects—those on the calling card.

Basic Activity

1. One child is designated as the caller. The other children each select a Bingo card and place it in front of them.

2. The caller turns over a calling card and shows it to the other children.

3. If the children have one or more of the matching quantities or numerals on their Bingo cards, they cover those squares with a lima bean.

4. Play continues until one child makes a complete row or, more commonly, until all the children have covered all of their squares. With only 10 calling cards, the turn-around time is pretty brief.

Extensions and Variations

Children comfortable with larger numbers can use Bingo and calling cards that go up to 20.

Concept and Skill Being Learned

- Matching numerals to quantities.

ADVICE COLUMN

The goal of this activity and others like it is to move children away from needing objects or pictures of objects to understand quantity. In chapter 1, children matched a set of 3 objects with another set of 3 objects. In this chapter, we have progressed to matching the numeral 3 with a set of 3 objects. A small step for adults, but a giant leap for children.

Number-Numeral Mystery Bag I

for TWO or MORE children

Materials and Setup

- ☐ Numeral cards, 0 to 10 (see page 13)
- ☐ Ten objects
- ☐ Mystery bag (see page 27 for more information)

Basic Activity

1 One child puts a secret number of objects in the mystery bag.

2 The second child feels in the bag and decides how many objects are in the bag.

3 The second child selects a numeral card to indicate how many objects he thinks are in the bag.

4 The objects are removed from the bag and counted to see if the chosen numeral is correct.

Extensions and Variations

Periodically change the objects in the mystery bag. For young children, if it feels different, it's a different activity.

Concept and Skill Being Learned

- Matching numerals to quantities. This time, children use their sense of touch to make the match.

ADVICE COLUMN

Too often, we neglect the multisensory nature of children's learning. Placing the objects in the mystery bag helps children focus on the information coming from their fingertips, translating that information into a mental representation of quantity. The more ways they can understand quantities and connect that knowledge with the abstract symbol for the number, the better.

Number-Numeral Mystery Bag II

for **TWO** or **MORE** children

Materials and Setup

☐ Picture cards, 0 to 9 (see page 13)

☐ Wooden, plastic, or sandpaper numerals, 0 to 9. Most educational supply catalogs and craft stores offer a variety of options. Refrigerator magnets can also do in a pinch

☐ Mystery bag (see page 27 for more information)

Basic Activity

1 Children place the set of numerals in the mystery bag and turn the stack of picture cards upside down as a draw pile.

2 They take turns turning over a picture card and reaching into the bag to retrieve the corresponding numeral, using only their sense of touch.

Extensions and Variations

- Each child chooses a picture card, looks at it, and then turns it face down. One at a time, children retrieve their numerals from the mystery bag. Together, they say the name of each numeral pulled from the bag, at which point individual children reveal their picture cards.

- Instead of picture cards, children can use cards showing Ten Frames filled with 0 to 9 dots (see Ten Frames, pages 61–63).

Concept and Skill Being Learned

- Matching numerals to quantities, using sense of touch to make the match.

ADVICE COLUMN

To renew interest in this activity, occasionally use a digital camera to change the images on the picture cards (for example, take pictures of no buttons, one button, two buttons, etc.). Children can help select the objects they want pictured.

Feed the Squirrel

for **ONE** or **MORE** children

Materials and Setup

☐ Half-gallon milk carton, empty and thoroughly cleaned

☐ Cutout of a squirrel (see page 217), colored and decorated. Attach the squirrel cutout to the front of the carton. The mouth of the squirrel should be cut out so the squirrel can be fed

☐ Bowl of acorns or nuts. Plastic substitutes can be used if you have reason to be concerned about allergies

☐ Numeral cards, 1 to 10 (see page 13)

Basic Activity

1 Children draw numeral cards from the deck and feed the squirrel that quantity of nuts.

Extensions and Variations

• Make this activity a group game. One child draws a card and looks at it without showing it to anyone else. That child feeds the squirrel the correct number of nuts, and the other children try to guess what card the child is holding.

• For children who know higher numerals, provide a set of numeral cards that go up to 20.

Concepts and Skills Being Learned

• Recognizing numerals.

• Associating quantities with numerals.

ADVICE COLUMN

This is a popular and versatile game. Seasonal variations can be used to renew children's interest in it. If you change the appearance of the game, children consider it entirely new.

Ten Frame Twister

Materials and Setup

☐ Large vinyl floor mat. You can use a shower curtain, window shade, or tarp. On the floor mat, make ten 8-inch squares in a Ten Frame arrangement (that is, 2 rows of 5 squares—see Ten Frames, pages 61–63), using a permanent marker, masking tape, or colored plastic tape. From left to right, write the numerals 1 to 5 in the top row of squares. Write the numerals 6 to 10 in the bottom row

☐ Numeral cards, 1 to 10 (see page 13)

Basic Activity

1 One child draws a numeral card from the deck and announces the number.

2 The second child places one foot in the corresponding Ten Frame square. The first child checks to make sure the second child is in the correct square, and then sets the numeral card down, face up.

3 The first child continues to draw cards. Each time, the other child tries to put a hand, foot, or other body part in the corresponding square without removing body parts from any of the previous squares.

4 The turn ends when the second child falls down or can't reach the called number without abandoning one of the previous squares.

5 The children switch roles and continue.

Extensions and Variations

• Use cards with picture icons rather than numerals.

• Cover the numerals on the Ten Frame mat with paper plates. The child takes a card from the deck and lifts the plate she thinks covers the matching numeral. When she finds the correct square, she places the numeral card on the plate. The children take turns, continuing until all the numeral cards have been placed.

Concepts and Skills Being Learned

- Numeral recognition.
- The relative position of the numerals 1 to 10 on the Ten Frame, using 5 and 10 as anchors.

ADVICE COLUMN

Too often we think small when creating materials for the classroom. If there's one thing we know about children, it's that they like to move. When children use their whole bodies, rather than just their eyes and hands, they have another way to relate to mathematics.

Number Art

Materials and Setup

- ☐ Paper, white or colored
- ☐ Art materials for collage making (scraps from magazines, bits of colored paper, feathers, yarn, beads, etc.)
- ☐ Scissors
- ☐ Glue
- ☐ Writing implement
- ☐ Die or spinner with numerals 5 to 10 (See page 164 for suggestions on how to make dice and spinners)

Basic Activity

1 Children each roll or spin.

2 They select that number of collage items to glue to the page in a pleasing arrangement. If they wish, they can draw additional details on the page.

3 They write the appropriate numeral below their masterpieces. They can also title what they have created.

Extensions and Variations

- Children can bind the collection of pages they have made into a book.
- A group of children can make a class book for the library shelf. Each child can contribute a collage for one of the numbers 5 through 10, or the children can create an entire book for each number—*The Book of 5*—with each child contributing a collage for that number.

Concepts and Skills Being Learned

- Recognizing numerals.
- Associating quantities with numerals.
- Writing numerals.
- Seeing quantities in a variety of contexts.

ADVICE COLUMN

The opportunities for exploring numeracy in art go well beyond this structured activity. Art is another means by which children think and communicate, and quantity is often an aspect of the reality they try to represent in their art. Look for opportunities to have conversations with children when they are designing, creating, and talking about their representations. For example, you could say,

- "Wow, that sure is a lot of trees. I wonder how many there are?"

- "So you have how many buttons on your shirt? Is that how many you drew in your picture?"

- "If you add two more scarecrows, how many would you have?"

- "So which of the houses you drew has more windows?"

However, keep in mind that not all preschoolers' art is at the representational stage. Their artistic creations may be purely experiential rather than something that can be identified and named. Don't push children to give a title to their creations: let that come from them. You can still ask mathematics-related questions, though: "Which scrap of paper is bigger?" "How many different colors did you use?"

The Literature Connection

COMMERCIAL
PRODUCT

ADVICE COLUMN

These books go beyond displaying a numeral with a quantity; in them, children must be able to read the numeral to know how many objects to look for in the pictures. It's best to read this kind of book to small groups or put them in the reading corner for children to read to themselves. The children need lots of time to scan the pictures, looking for the named objects.

Anno, Mitsumasa. 1975. *Anno's Counting Book*. New York: Harper & Row.

Brocklehurst, Ruth. 2002. *1001 Animals to Spot*. London: Usborne.

Carle, Eric. 1974. *My Very First Book of Numbers*. New York: Scholastic.

Daynes, Katie. 2003. *1001 Things to Spot in the Sea*. London: Usborne.

Doherty, Gillian. 1999. *1001 Things to Spot on the Farm*. London: Usborne.

Helbrough, Emma. 2005. *1001 Bugs to Spot*. London: Usborne.

Murphy, Stuart. 1997. *Everybody Counts*. New York: HarperCollins.

Spafford, Suzy. 2002. *Witzy's Numbers*. New York: Scholastic.

6

emergence of part-whole awareness

I consider this chapter the most important one in this book because it describes the kind of math practice most needed, and most often lacking, when children move beyond simple counting. Their next great leap in number awareness is the ability to take numbers apart and put them back together again in their heads, not just with their hands.

We have to be careful not to expect this skill of children before it develops naturally, which is what we do if we rush them into addition and subtraction work. Without a strong foundation of the skills in the previous chapters, children not only *can't* take numbers apart and put them back together, they don't even believe *it's possible* to do so.

Children start out thinking that once a quantity has been fiddled with, it is no longer the same quantity. Once they understand that quantities can be conserved, they are able to break a quantity into 2 pieces, realize the total quantity is still the same, and then conclude that those 2 pieces, combined, equal the total.

You know children are ready for the activities in this chapter if

- they don't re-count a set of objects when you rearrange the objects and ask them, "How many are there now?"

- they can count forward and backward from starting points other than 1

- when finding the difference between two numbers (for example, 6 and 8), they start from one number and count toward the other (for example, "Six . . . seven, eight—that's two.")

- they use strategies other than random guessing to determine the missing part of a whole

Once children understand part-whole relationships, they start looking at all the ways numbers can be disassembled and reassembled. They start to see patterns— say, that 2 plus 4 makes 6, and so does 4 plus 2 (in other words, the commutative property, which states that the order of the numbers being added does not affect the sum). They also start to remember certain combinations. They may become fascinated by doubles facts (for example, that 4 and 4 equals 8). They also develop some handy tools for moving through numeric space, such as

- Counting on. When children add one quantity to another (for example, 3 plus 2), they don't need to re-count the first quantity to figure out the total ("One, two, three, four, five!"). Instead, they count on from the starting quantity ("Three . . . four, five! Five!"). This is a big time saver.

- Counting back. When children know how many they started with (for example, 6) and they know how many were taken away (for example, 2), they don't need to count the quantity that remains ("One, two, three, four! Four!"). Instead, they count backward from the starting quantity ("Six, five, four. Four!"). This skill is especially useful as the numbers get bigger.

- Counting on from the larger quantity. If the children are adding 2 quantities, they start their count from the larger one. For example, if one child has 2 marbles and a second child gives her 5 more, she doesn't count "Two . . . three, four, five, six, seven." Instead, she counts "Five . . . six, seven. Now I've got seven."

Chapter 6 is filled with activities to help children explore part-whole relationships. The more time children spend on these activities, the easier they'll find math later on. As you've probably guessed by now, children who can confidently relate parts to wholes already understand how to add and subtract.

Hand Game II

Materials and Setup

☐ 3 to 10 Unifix cubes (which work well because they snap together), or any small manipulatives such as lima beans or beads that are all the same color

Basic Activity

1 Children decide on the quantity to work with, snap that number of Unifix cubes together (or gather that number of manipulatives), and set the remaining ones aside.

2 The first child holds the manipulatives behind his back and separates them into 2 groups, holding 1 group in each hand.

3 The child brings 1 hand in front of his body and opens it to reveal its contents: "I had ____. Here I have ____. How many are still behind my back?"

4 The second child guesses, and the first child shows his other hand, revealing the missing portion: "It was ____, because ____ (showing the original set) and ____ (showing the set just revealed) makes ____ (snaps or groups the 2 sets together to make the original amount)."

5 Children continue the game, taking turns.

Extensions and Variations

- Encourage children to sometimes keep all the contents in one hand, making 0 the correct guess for the contents of the other hand.

- Include a double set of numeral cards. Children find the numeral representing the whole quantity and keep it displayed throughout the game. The first child reveals the first part, and the second child finds the appropriate numeral card to set next to the revealed quantity. The second child then selects the numeral she thinks matches the missing quantity, and the first child shows his other hand.

- The first child divides the whole into more than two parts. He then reveals all the parts but one before asking the second child to guess what part is still missing.

- Children can play a more-less-same game using manipulatives small enough to be hidden in a closed fist (beans or beads work well for this activity). The children choose a quantity to work with. The first child puts that many manipulatives in one hand, puts his hands behind his back, and transfers some of the manipulatives to the other hand. He then holds both fists out in front of him. The second child taps one of the hands, and the first child reveals its contents. The first child then asks, "Do you think the other hand holds more, less, or the same?" The second child guesses, and then the first child opens his other hand. They discuss whether the second amount was in fact more, less, or the same as the original.

Concepts and Skills Being Learned

- Part-whole relationships.

- The concept of 0.

- The concept of more, less, and same.

- This activity is also early preparation for understanding addition and subtraction.

ADVICE COLUMN

Until the part-whole concept firmly establishes itself in children's minds, they tend to treat this type of activity as a guessing game rather than as something they can predict with accuracy. For this reason, don't have them start with too high a number. You'll be amazed how difficult it is for them to think about the amount not seen. Once you see them answering confidently and accurately on a consistent basis, you can encourage them to use larger quantities to challenge themselves.

Also pay attention to how children are coming up with their answers. They might be

- counting the first quantity and then counting on from there, perhaps keeping track of the counts on their fingers. For example, if a stack of 6 cubes is being used and 4 are revealed, they might count the seen quantity: "One, two, three, four . . . " and then keep counting up to the target quantity: " . . . five (raising one finger), six (raising a second finger)." They then count the raised fingers and guess "Two!"

- counting on from the first quantity *without* re-counting that quantity. In this case, they look at the revealed 4 and count, "Five, six," raising a finger with each count. They then count the raised fingers and guess: "Two!" Note that this is a more advanced skill. The children realize that counting does not need to start from 1 if one part of the whole has already been named.

- counting backward from the whole amount to the amount seen (version one). In this version, the children hold up 6 fingers and lower 1 finger at a time as they count the visible set: "One, two, three, four." They then count the remaining raised fingers and guess: "Two!"

- counting backward from the whole amount to the amount seen (version two). This is a more sophisticated version than the previous approach. Here they verbally count backward once for each cube in the revealed set, keeping track of the backward counts on their fingers: "Five (looking at the first cube and raising one finger), four (looking at the second cube and raising a second finger), three (looking at the third cube and raising a third finger), two (looking at the final cube and raising a fourth finger)—two." What they are doing is mentally removing one cube at a time from the original set. This is why children start their counts at 5 rather than at the original quantity, 6. For a long time, children cannot do this correctly. They count the starting point as 1 instead of 0. This makes all their counts off by 1.

- remembering the math fact. They know that 4 and 2 make 6. In their heads, they're thinking, "If the whole is six, and four is seen, then the missing part must be two." Is this subtraction? Maybe—they might be thinking $6 - 4 = 2$. Is it addition? Again, maybe—they might be thinking $4 + \underline{\qquad} = 6$. We don't know which one they are thinking unless we ask them, and even then, they may not be able to verbalize the mental strategy being used.

All of these strategies suggest that children believe the total quantity hasn't been changed by the action. In Piagetian terms, they are demonstrating *conservation*. This means they are starting to emerge from their senses-based, pre-operational stage of development into the next and more logic-based concrete operational stage. Children who are pre-operational believe that a set of 8 pennies becomes more pennies when they are spread out and that the same set becomes fewer pennies when they are tightly clustered. Even after such children count both sets and tell you that both total 8, they insist there are more pennies in the spread-out arrangement. In other words, they still believe the evidence of their senses more than the abstract concept of 8. Until children reach the concrete operational stage, they need to recount a set each time it changes before they can tell you how many there are. But even then, the number they tell you is just a name to them, not a stable attribute of the set. Ask them which of two sets is more. You'll see that they'll look, not count.

Cover Up

Materials and Setup

☐ Set of 3 to 10 flat manipulatives, such as pennies or lima beans

☐ A piece of tagboard or cloth to serve as an opaque cover

Basic Activity

1 Children decide on the quantity of manipulatives to work with and set the remaining ones aside.

2 The first child closes her eyes or turns her back while the second child slips some of the manipulatives under the cover.

3 The first child opens her eyes, looks at the visible set, and guesses how many manipulatives are under the cover.

4 The second child reveals how many manipulatives were under the cover, and the first child verifies her guess.

5 The children switch roles and continue.

Extensions and Variations

• For a larger group of children, provide an overhead projector. With the projector on, the first child places a certain quantity on the projector screen for the other children to see and count, and then turns the projector off. With the projector off, the same child uses the cover to hide part of the quantity. The child turns on the projector to show the portion of the set still visible. The other children guess the missing amount. The first child then removes the cover and reveals the missing amount.

• For children who can write their numerals, same as the above version, but provide children in the audience with response boards on which to secretly record their guesses. Chalkboards or erasable boards make good response boards, but children can also use plain sheets of paper. For those who know their numerals but cannot write them, provide a set of numeral cards with which they can display their guess. The children record their guesses, and then the first child lifts the cover. The rest then reveal their guesses and compare them to the actual amount that was hidden. Note this is an interesting twist on the original game: the missing amount is revealed before the children show their guesses to each other.

Concepts and Skills Being Learned

- Part-whole relationships.

- Counting on or counting back. Two of the strategies children might be using are counting upward from the visible set to the target number (for example, if the original set was 7, and 4 are now showing, the children might count from the 4 (". . . five, six, seven") or from the original quantity to the quantity seen (for example, " . . . six, five, four"). This is not as easy as you might think, because both strategies require them to keep track of how many counts they take, not the number names that are being said (for example, the correct answer to the above problem is three, but in neither strategy do children ever say "three" while counting). Both of these are essential skills to develop and signal that the children are developing a mature number sense.

ADVICE COLUMN

You might say of this and some of the upcoming activities, "Hey, isn't that the same as the last activity you shared?" To the adult mind, these activities are quite similar because they call for the same skill. But preschool children do not experience the world as we do. Their world is very concrete. If the props and the actions change, it's a new experience. Our goal is to have the children keep practicing the same skill while we keep changing the context required for it. Cognitive psychologists call this *generalization*, and it is a vital step in making an idea or skill truly useful.

Bears in a Cave

Materials and Setup

- [ ] 3 to 10 plastic counting bears, all the same color. Counting bears are a popular math manipulative found in most educational supply catalogs. Other manipulative characters can be substituted—you just need to change the story to fit the props

- [ ] Opaque box or small storage bin—the box is set upside down and has a cutout to serve as the entrance to the bears' cave (see photo)

Basic Activity

1. Children decide how many bears to work with and set the remaining bears aside.

2. The first time you introduce this activity to them, share the following story with the children:

   "These bears are on a picnic. They've decided to play a special game of hide-and-seek and they would like *you* to be It. You're going to close your eyes and cover them with your hands, and while your eyes are closed the bears are going to move. Some of the bears are going to stay out where you can see them but some of them are going to hide in the cave. When you hear 'Ready,' you can open your eyes and try to guess how many bears are hiding in the cave."

3. While the first child hides his eyes, the second child puts some of the bears in the cave, rearranges the others, and says "Ready."

4. After the first child guesses how many bears are in the cave, the cave is lifted, and the children count the hidden bears together.

Extensions and Variations

- Encourage children to occasionally leave all of the bears out in the open or put all of them in the cave. This forces the children to think about 0 as a quantity.

- Children can play a version of the game in which the objective is to guess the total number of bears. In this version, the first child closes his eyes while the second child puts the supply of bears behind her back. While the first child's eyes are closed, the second child selects the number of bears to put out, placing some of them where they can be seen and some in the cave. When the first child opens his eyes, the second child announces: "There are _____ bears hiding in the cave." The first child has to guess the total number of bears.

Concepts and Skills Being Learned

- Part-whole relationships.
- Concept of 0.

ADVICE COLUMN

Putting mathematical concepts into the context of a story is a very powerful teaching strategy. Children can demonstrate unexpectedly sophisticated skills when the context makes sense to them. That's one of the reasons literature is such a valuable addition to a math curriculum. Dramatic play, felt boards, and so on are valuable tools for embedding mathematical ideas in meaningful contexts. Try to incorporate math into stories and dramatic play as often as you can to expand children's mathematical understandings.

Believe it or not, young children are so visual that if you don't rearrange the bears that remain outside the cave, some of them will visualize the original scene and count the empty spaces where the hidden bears were and then tell you how many are missing. In my Montessori training, I was taught this: "Young children take photographs. Older children draw sketches." This means that young children tend to remember scenes literally, in all their particulars, rather than deciding which aspects are worth remembering. Older children and adults focus on the information they are trying to remember (for example, the number of bears) and forget less relevant details, such as where the bears stood originally. Females are supposed to have better memories for visual detail than males. That might be why I find this phenomenon so spooky!

This brings up another important point: young children have a hard time describing the quantity *not* present (for example, if there were 7 bears originally and 4 were hidden, it is difficult for them to think about the 4 in the cave rather than the 3 they can actually see). This is why children are more likely to count upward from the visible set to the whole than to count backward from the whole to the visible set. It is also what makes subtraction harder for children than addition.

Shaker Boxes

Materials and Setup

☐ Small cardboard box with a removable lid, marked with a numeral on the lid to show how many counters are inside

☐ Counters with two distinctive sides (for example, pennies, counting discs with differently colored sides, lima beans painted red on one side). Start with as few as 3 objects and go up to as many as 7 or 8 (see photo)

Basic Activity

1 The children check to make sure the number of counters in the box matches the numeral written on the lid.

2 The first child vigorously shakes the box, opens the lid, and sorts the contents into 2 groups.

3 The first child tells the second child, "I have _____ red beans. How many white beans do you think I have?"

4 The second child guesses, and the first child verifies the answer by looking in the box.

Extensions and Variations

- To make the shaker boxes more versatile, cover the lid with an erasable material, such as contact paper or wipe-off posterboard sheets, available at some craft stores. In setting up the game, children can select how many objects to put in the box and write that numeral on the lid. Alternatively, you can provide a set of Velcro numerals so the children can attach the appropriate numeral to the lid.

- Provide a recording sheet that shows multiple rows of beans, with the number of beans in each row equaling the target number on the shaker box. After each trial, a child records the results by coloring the appropriate number of beans in the row. For children who know their numerals, you can add 2 blank boxes under each row of beans where the children can write the numeral for how many of each group they counted (see illustration on the next page). For example, if they counted 5 red beans and 2 white beans, they would fill in 5 and 2. (Don't use the + and = sign symbols. These symbols have no meaning for children at this age.) Children can gather the pages from all of their trials with a particular shaker box (the 7, for instance) and staple them together into a book titled *My Book of 7.*

- Provide manipulatives that can be divided into 3 parts (for example, red, white, and blue by using red/white beans and blue/white beans) or 4 parts (for example, red, blue, green, and yellow by using red/blue beans and green/yellow beans). The first child announces all but one of the colors, and the second child guesses the missing amount.

Concepts and Skills Being Learned

- Part-whole relationships.
- The concept of 0.
- This activity is also a first step toward recording addition and subtraction facts.

ADVICE COLUMN

You can use silent materials in the shaker boxes, like bicolored foam discs, to cut down on classroom noise. But part of the appeal of activities like this one is the noisy rattling of the materials when they're shaken. Sometimes we place too much emphasis on classrooms being quiet places. Make sure your decisions about limiting classroom noise are based on the children's needs, not your own.

Don't have children write the traditional number sentence yet (3 + 4 = 7). There is time for that later. Research has shown that children attach very little meaning to formal arithmetical expressions until they have had lots of experience exploring the underlying number relationships. In fact, researchers have found that children in the early grades usually come up with a written equation only after they have solved the problem, not as a way to solve the problem.

Toothpick Designs

Materials and Setup

☐ Box of flat wooden toothpicks. Toothpicks are inexpensive so they are a good choice for this activity, but if you believe your children are too young to handle them safely, you can provide larger objects, such as coffee stirrers, cotton ear swabs, or short, thin strips of construction paper. Another interesting variation is to give the children flexible pieces, such as short pieces of yarn or pipe cleaner, with which to make their constructions

☐ Numeral cards, 3 to 10 (see page 13)

Basic Activity

1 Children each choose a numeral card.

2 They count out the number of toothpicks specified on the numeral card and arrange them to form a design or image. They can also name this creation.

3 They count out another set of the same number of toothpicks and place them in a different arrangement.

4 They continue making new arrangements of the same quantity until they cannot think of another way to arrange that number of toothpicks.

Extensions and Variations

- Each child glues his arrangements onto separate sheets of paper, and then gathers the sheets into a book titled *My Book of [the number]*. The book can then be stapled or hole-punched and sewn with yarn.

- Have every child in the class make a design using the same quantity of objects. The children can then tour the classroom to look at each other's creations. Or they can glue their creations on paper, write their names on them, and turn them into a class wall display.

- Have children make the first initial of their names with the toothpicks. You can then lead a discussion about how many used three toothpicks, how many used four, and so on. They can create a graph using their creations to show how many initials can be made from three toothpicks, how many from four, etc.

- Ask each child, "How did you make that?" As they mention each part of their creations, you can ask, "How many toothpicks did you use to make that part?" When you have discussed all the parts, you can summarize as you point to each part: "So you used two . . . and two . . . and two . . . and one to make seven."

Concepts and Skills Being Learned

- Part-whole relationships.
- Quantity needed to make specific images and designs (for example, some designs are possible with 4 toothpicks that aren't possible with 3).

ADVICE COLUMN

By limiting children to a particular number of toothpicks before they begin their creations, you force them to look at the relationship between their design ideas and the quantity of pieces available. In a non-coercive way, you are engaging them in problem solving about quantity.

This is one of the best activities I know of for convincing children that a given quantity can look many different ways. You might find a child who decides to break a toothpick in half in order to use one part in one location and the second part in another. Talking about whether that is allowed and whether the broken toothpick is still 1 or now 2 can lead to interesting conversations about fractions.

Domino Sorting

Materials and Setup

☐ Commercial set of dominoes

☐ Numeral cards, 0 to 12 (see page 13)

Basic Activity

1 Children arrange the numeral cards in order from 0–12, left to right.

2 They place dominoes under the numeral cards that correspond to the total number of dots on the domino (for example, a domino that has 6 dots on one half and 3 on the other half is placed under the 9 numeral card).

Extensions and Variations

- Younger children can find all the dominoes that have one quantity (say, 5) on one half or the other. Or you can provide multiple sets of dominoes, and children can find the dominoes that match.

- Create a small mat using laminated tagboard or cardboard. Recycled shower curtains or window shades can also be cut into mats. On the mat, write the numerals 0 to 12 across the bottom. Above each numeral, trace domino outlines in a vertical fashion so that you have columns made up of 10 rectangles above each numeral (see illustration). The child then places dominoes above the numerals according to the total number of dots on each domino. **Note:** Once all the dominoes are in place, an interesting visual pattern emerges—the end columns have just one domino, the central columns have eight. But because all the columns are 10 rectangles high, the children aren't forced by the mat's design to come up with the correct sums.

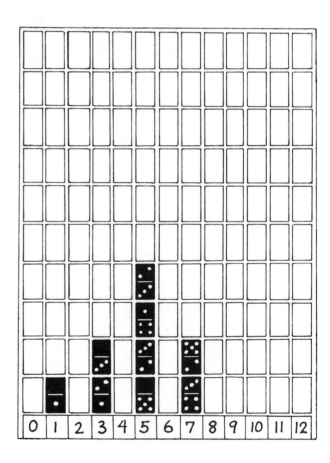

- Children sort their dominoes according to the total number of dots (for example, all the dominoes with 7 dots are placed in one group). Within each group, children then arrange the dominoes in a patterned sequence (for example, they can arrange dominoes with a total of 7 dots in the following sequence: 1–6, 2–5, 3–4, 4–3, 5–2, 6–1).

- Children record the different combinations of the dots on all the dominoes under each numeral card, either by drawing the dominoes or by writing the pairs of numerals.

- They use the *difference* between the quantity of dots on the 2 sides to determine what group the domino belongs in. For instance, they would place both the 5–2 domino and the 3–0 domino in the same pile.

- They can make domino trains that add up to 10 or some other quantity. For instance, the child could make a 10-train using the 1–2 and 3–4 dominoes or by using the 2–2, 4–0, and 1–1.

- Provide dominoes with up to 9 dots or up to 15 dots on each piece (these are commercial products that are available in many retail outlets). Children can explore part-whole relationships with these larger sums.

- Make your own domino set using tagboard or 1 inch x 1 inch counting tiles glued together. Variations include

  - drawing the dots in random, unpatterned arrangements. This forces children to pay attention to the quantity rather the visual pattern of dots

  - making a set in which one side has a dot arrangement and the other has a numeral

- Play "Domino Concentration." Provide a partial domino set of 8 to 12 pieces, using pairs of dominoes with the same sums (2–0 and 1–1; 2–5 and 1–6; 3–3 and 6–0). Children start with all the dominoes face down and take turns flipping over 2 at a time. If the dominoes match, they keep the trick; if not, they flip them back face down and the next child takes a turn.

- Play "Domino Go Fish." Provide a partial domino set of 20 dominoes, with 4 dominoes each for the sums of 4 through 8 (for the sum of 4, you could put in 4–0, 3–1, 1–3, and 2–2). Children start with 4 dominoes standing upright in front of them and the rest of the dominoes face down in a draw pile. They take turns, asking others if they have any more of one of the dominoes they hold in their hand (for example, "Do you have any fives?"). If the child asked has any of that sum, she gives them to the child who asked; if not, she says, "Go Fish," and the first child pulls a domino from the draw pile. Once a child has 4 of the same sum, he can lay the trick down. Play continues until all the sets have been laid down.

- Play "Domino Bingo." Create bingo cards in a 5 x 5 configuration with dominoes pictured in all squares so that there are no duplicate sums within any column. (See illustration on the next page.) For younger children, use only the smaller sums. Create calling cards with the letters *B*, *I*, *N*, *G*, and *O*, and each of the sums that are used on the cards (for example, B–8, N–5, G–5, I–9). The caller reads one card at a time, and the players mark their cards with a counter if they have the matching sum under the appropriate letter. The game ends when all the children have made 5 in a row or have filled up their entire cards. **Note:** For an easier version, use dominoes as the calling cards, and make Bingo cards with the numeral sums listed in the squares.

Concepts and Skills Being Learned

- Part-whole relationships.
- Different quantity combinations can add up to the same sum.
- Patterns in the number combinations that make up a sum.
- Preparation for learning addition and subtraction facts.

ADVICE COLUMN

Fancy sets of dominoes, color-coded by quantity, are available on the market. I prefer the black-and-white variety, which in their plainness help ensure that children focus on quantities rather than on colors. If you do purchase a color-coded set, consider coloring all of the dots black before you use them in the classroom.

Workjobs Mats

Materials and Setup

- [ ] Workjobs mats. These mats show scenes, such as a beach, an apple orchard, or a farm. The scenes can be hand drawn or cut from magazines. You can make the mats using tagboard or cardboard. Create multiple mats on which the same scene is pictured. In choosing magazine photos or thinking about what to draw, choose scenes that have at least two separate areas on which a set of suitable manipulative objects can easily fit. For example, you might create 4 mats showing the same waterfront scene with a beach area and a water area, and use seashells as the manipulatives. Another set might show an apple tree, with toy apples provided that can be placed either on the tree or in the basket. A third set might include cutouts of bees hovering over flowers or outside their hive

- [ ] Sets of manipulatives to go with the mats. Have enough for up to 10 items on each mat

- [ ] Numeral cards, 4 to 10 (see page 13)

- [ ] Boxes to store the sets. Donated pizza boxes make nice containers in which to store sets of mats and manipulatives

Basic Activity

1. Children choose a numeral from the deck of cards to set above the mats.

2. They take the first mat, choose the indicated number of manipulatives, and arrange them in the two portions of the scene.

3. They repeat this activity with the matching mats, each time using the same quantity but making a different arrangement.

Extensions and Variations

- As children finish each arrangement, they can use numeral cards to label how many manipulatives they have in each of the 2 parts of scene. You may need to provide additional numeral card sets for this extension.

- Use scenes with more than 2 places to put manipulatives.

- Ask questions, such as,
    - "How many seashells did you put on the beach on this mat?"
    - "Which mat has more seashells on the beach?"
    - "How many more seashells are on the beach in this picture than in this one?"

Concept and Skill Being Learned

- Part-whole relationships.

ADVICE COLUMN

Workjobs is the name given by Mary Baratta-Lorton to some activities that extended her classic work. Like the activity described here, she posed hands-on, part-whole problems in contexts that were meaningful to children. Her books *Workjobs* and *Workjobs II* are still available from Dale Seymour Publications. *Box It or Bag It Mathematics* (Math Learning Center, 1988) is another popular resource that exercises similar skills.

How Many All Together?

Materials and Setup

- ☐ Deck of playing cards, face cards removed
- ☐ Beans or other small manipulatives
- ☐ Opaque cup

Basic Activity

1. Shuffle the deck of cards.

2. The first child draws a card, counts out the appropriate quantity of beans, and places the beans in the cup.

3. The same child then covers the top of the cup with the playing card, face up, so the beans are not visible.

4. The second child draws a card, counts out that quantity of beans, and places them in front of the cup, along with the card drawn.

5. Children try to guess how many beans they have all together.

6. Children pour out the beans and count the total.

Extensions and Variations

- Children use a spinner, die, or some other method (for example, tossing beanbags or rings at numeral targets) to generate the second number. (See page 164 for how to make your own spinners and dice.)

- Before children count the correct answer, encourage them to talk to each other about how they came up with it. For example, you could ask, "How did you figure out so quickly that your five beans in the cup and the four beans on the table would make nine?" "I counted." "But how could you count? You couldn't see some of the beans." "But I knew it was five, so I just kept counting—six, seven, eight, nine. See? Nine."

- For younger children, use only the cards 1 to 5, so the sums don't go above 10.

Concepts and Skills Being Learned

- Part-whole relationships.

- Counting on. Because one of the parts is invisible, children cannot simply count all the beans to make their guess. In the exchange above, the child was encouraged by the design of the task to use the numeral representing the hidden quantity as a starting number (for example, 5), counting the visible beans upward from that point (" . . . six, seven, eight, nine—I guess nine."). Of course, children can also count from one up to the numeral sitting on top of the cup ("One, two, three, four, five . . .") and keep counting the visible set from there (" . . . six, seven, eight, nine—I guess nine."). In fact, it is by initially solving the problem this way that they convince themselves that re-counting the starting set is a waste of time. When they reach this conclusion, they have achieved an understanding of conservation of quantity. (See the advice column in Hand Game II on pages 113–115.) Counting on is an important milestone for children. It means they can mentally manipulate quantities rather than physically count them.

ADVICE COLUMN

Children tend to rush past the thinking part of this activity, each shouting out a guess and quickly dumping out the beans to count the total. Encourage them to pause and really think about the quantities represented by the two cards displayed. That's one of the reasons you ask them questions about their guesses before they check them—so they actually have a reason behind their guess. Being confident that they know the answer and having their reasoning validated when they count the beans is much more fulfilling than simply being lucky.

Disappearing Act

Materials and Setup

☐ Ten pennies or other flat counters

☐ Two sets of numeral cards, 1 to 10 (see page 13)

☐ 10 cm x 20 cm (4 inch x 8 inch) tagboard card. The right half of the card has a 10 cm x 10 cm (4 inch x 4 inch) tagboard flap attached along the top edge. This flap is used to hide the manipulatives on the right side of the card until it is time to reveal them

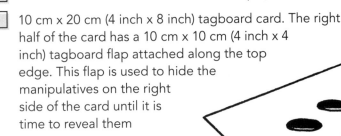

Basic Activity

1 Start with the flap covering the right side of the card.

2 The first child selects how many flat counters to put on the left side of the card.

3 The first child finds the numeral card that equals the total number of counters and places it above the card.

4 While the first child looks away, the second child slides some of the counters under the flap, making sure they are covered.

5 The first child then counts the visible counters, selects the matching numeral card, and places it below the left side of the card.

6 The first child then predicts how many counters are under the flap by selecting another numeral card and placing it below the right side of the card.

7 The second child lifts the flap to let the first child see if the prediction was correct.

8 The children switch roles, keeping the same base quantity.

Extensions and Variations

Instead of using a flap, use a tray or baking pan, face down, to cover the right-hand portion of the card. (This activity is then very similar to Cover Up on pages 116–117 and Bears in a Cave on pages 118–119.)

Easier versions:

- Do the activity without the numeral cards.

- Provide additional counters and a second 10 cm x 20 cm (4 inch x 8 inch) card. On this card, instead of using a flap, draw a line down the middle. This card is used by the child who is guessing. He can put counters on this work mat to decide how many pennies are under the flap. The mat allows the child to manipulate objects while they are being counted rather than having to visualize those that are covered.

Harder version:

- Make the game card 10 cm x 30 cm (4 inch x 12 inch) with three flaps, so that any of the three parts of the card can be covered. After the initial quantity is selected, the first child distributes the quantity to each of the three sections, keeping two of the three flaps open. The second child then has to decide how many counters are hidden under the third flap.

Concepts and Skills Being Learned

- Part-whole relationships.

- Counting on.

- Counting back from the starting quantity to the visible quantity. This is a common and useful strategy for children to develop.

ADVICE COLUMN

Of course, children can choose to change the base quantity each time, but doing so diminishes their experience of exploring how a given quantity can be subdivided. Encourage them to stick instead with rearranging the same quantity. They are more likely to enjoy success this way, which in turn helps them grow more confident in their abilities.

Handfuls Game I

Materials and Setup

☐ Basket of manipulatives small enough that young hands can hold 10 to 15 of them

☐ More/Less spinner (spinner with *More* written on one half and *Less* on the other. You can use picture icons, such as an elephant on one side and a mouse on the other, to help young children remember which is which. See page 210 for a template.)

☐ Scoreboard with 4 or more columns, 20 spaces per column

Basic Activity

1 Each child grabs a handful of manipulatives and counts them.

2 One child spins the More/Less spinner.

3 Children compare their quantities to see who has the largest and smallest amounts.

4 The child with the most/least gets to put the difference between their quantity and their next closest competitor's quantity on the scoreboard (so, for example, in 2-person play, if the first child has 12 counters, the second child has 15 counters, and the spinner comes up *Less*, the first child adds 3 counters to his column on the scoreboard).

5 Game ends when one child's column on the scoreboard is filled.

Extensions and Variations

A simpler version of the game: the child who has more/less wins the turn. Children can tally how many turns they have won, if they wish (Handfuls Game II on page 159).

Concepts and Skills Being Learned

• Relative size of numbers.

• Counting on and counting back.

• The comparison method of subtraction (also known as the *missing addend method of addition*). Some children need to line up their manipulatives side-by-side to see how many don't have a match in order to determine how much more one quantity is than the other.

ADVICE COLUMN

The More/Less spinner, an innovation dating back to Mary Baratta-Lorton's *Mathematics Their Way* curriculum, is not necessary, but it provides a nice touch. It helps deliver the much-needed message to today's children that more is not always better. Besides, it keeps children in suspense for a moment—even after they have counted their quantities, they still don't know who has won.

This is a slightly different task from most of the others in this section because it does not involved subdividing a given quantity. Still, the act of comparing one quantity to another and finding the difference helps children conceptualize the smaller number as a part of the larger one.

Parts-of Puzzle Cards

for **ONE** *or* **MORE** children

Materials and Setup

Tagboard puzzle pieces. These are made up of two columns of squares in different combinations, each square filled in with a black dot. The pieces fit together to add up to a target number. As an example, the Parts-of-8 set contains the following puzzle pieces (pictured at right):

- a single square (the "one" puzzle piece)

- two squares side by side (the "two" puzzle piece)

- two squares in the first column, one in the second (the "three" puzzle piece)

- two squares in the first column, two in the second (the "four" puzzle piece)—you need *two* of these pieces

- three squares in the first column, two in the second (the "five" puzzle piece)

- three squares in the first column, three in the second (the "six" puzzle piece)

- four squares in the first column, three in the second (the "seven" puzzle piece)

- four squares in the first column, four in the second (the "eight" puzzle piece)

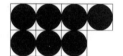
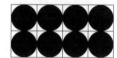

These nine puzzle pieces allow the child to make all the combinations of eight (8, 7+1, 6+2, 5+3, and 4+4). A template for these appears on page 207.

Basic Activity

1. A child locates the piece matching the target number of the set (for example, if this is the Parts-of-8 set, the child looks for the 8-piece). This piece is kept to compare with each of the other combinations they create.

2. The child then finds 2 other cards that, when put together, match the reference piece.

3. The child continues until all the pieces are matched up.

Extensions and Variations

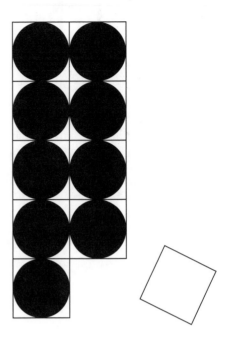

- Numerals can be written on the backs of the pieces (for example, on the 3-piece, you would write a 3). The child can see if she has counted the quantity accurately by flipping the piece over. She can also flip over both puzzle pieces to see the numeral combinations that add up to the target number.

- The child can be encouraged to verbalize the combinations (for example, "I used three and five to make eight.").

- The child can make the target quantity using 3 puzzle pieces.

- Include some puzzle pieces of numbers greater than the target number, along with eraser pieces—these puzzle pieces are made of gray squares that have *no* black dots in them. For example, you could add to the Parts-of-8 set the following pieces (pictured at right):

  - 5 squares in the first column, 4 in the second (a "nine" puzzle piece)

  - 5 squares in the first column, 5 in the second (a "ten" puzzle piece)

  - 1 gray square, with no dot in it (a 1-eraser piece)

  - 2 gray squares side by side, with no dots in them (a 2-eraser piece)

  The child can now make 2 additional combinations of 8 by covering up the top dot on the 9-dot puzzle piece with the 1-eraser (9 - 1) and covering the top row of the 10-dot puzzle piece with the 2-eraser (10 - 2). The child is, in effect, subtracting.

Concepts and Skills Being Learned

- Part-whole relationships, both additive and subtractive.

- Counting on and counting back.

- Odd numbers versus even numbers and their underlying properties. Children don't know the terms *odd* and *even*, but they do notice that some of the puzzle pieces have a pair of squares on the top (that is, they are even) and others have a single square on the top row (they have an odd square). As they search for pieces to fit together, they also prove some of the addition rules of odd and even numbers (for example, an even number can be made by combining two even numbers or by combining two odd numbers; an odd number can only be made by combining an odd number with an even number). Children do not need to know or to be able to articulate this rule, but they learn it as part of a broad and deep understanding of numbers over time, through hands-on problem solving.

ADVICE COLUMN

This manipulative set provides a striking visual demonstration of how different combinations of numbers add up to identical quantities (2 and 3 add up to 5, as do 1 and 4). Other manipulatives such as the Cuisenaire rods can be used to explore parts-of relationships, but often their combinations don't result in visually identical sets.

With many of these puzzle activities, children can mechanically assemble the pieces without ever pondering their numerical relationships. Only when they are attentive to the quantities they are manipulating do they deepen their mathematical understanding. Encouraging children to verbalize what they have done is one of the best ways of ensuring that this mental-processing step takes place. For example, you might ask,

- "How did you know which card to look for to go with the five?"

- "So that card is how many? How many more do you think you need to make eight?"

- "You made eight using which two cards?"

- "Is ten more than eight or less than eight? How much more? How do you know that?"

- "That one looks bigger than eight. I wonder how many it is."

- "Is there any way to make eight using three pieces?"

Flip Book

for ONE or MORE children

Materials and Setup

For this activity, make a flip book, which is a book where each page is cut vertically down the center. Each side of the split page shows icons that, when counted together, equal the target quantity for the book.

☐ To make the cover, cut a piece of 8.5 inch x 11 inch card stock or tagboard into thirds so that you have three 3.67 inch x 8.5 inch pieces. Use two of these pieces for the front and back covers. On the front cover, write *Book of 8* or whatever you decide to use as the target numeral.

☐ To make the interior pages, cut a sheet of 8.5 inch x 11 inch card stock into thirds as you did for the covers above. Then cut each of these sheets in half vertically so that you have six 3.67 inch x 4.25 inch pieces of paper. On each half, draw icons or place stickers that add up to the target numeral when the two sheets are put together. The icons on the two parts that form a pair should be different (for example, in the *Book of 8*, one of the left-hand pages could have 3 stars, and one of the right-hand pages could have 5 balloons). Include all the number combinations that add up to the target number (for example, 1 + 7, 2 + 6, 3 + 5, 4 + 4, 5 + 3, 6 + 2, 7 + 1). When assembling the book, randomly order the matching parts so that the first left-hand page does not make 8 when matched with the first right-hand page (see illustration).

☐ After you have all the pages of the book in the desired order, sew the book together along the top edge with yarn, or comb-bind it.

Basic Activity

1 The child chooses a flip book with the target number he wishes to practice.

2 The child selects any starting page on the left or the right side and counts how many icons are on it.

3 The child flips through the pages on the opposite side until he finds a page whose icons add up to the target number.

Extensions and Variations

- Provide manipulatives. The child can use them to help figure out the missing quantity and then find a page on the opposite side of the book with that number.

- Make a book in which, instead of splitting the card, you use a blank, opaque flap to cover up the right-hand side of the page. (The blank flap must be attached at the bottom or on the right-hand side of the back cover so it can be flipped independent of the pages.) The first child can find two pages that match up to the target number and use the flap to cover the right-hand side of the page. The second child then looks at the left-hand side and predicts what's under the flap (this activity is very similar to Disappearing Act, on pages 131–132).

- Provide a copy of the flip book that does not have its pages split for the second child to hold. While the first child works with the flip book, the second child locates the solution page. Once the first child has selected a matching set of pages, the second child reveals the answer.

- Make a flip book with numerals on one side and picture icons on the other. This encourages the child to use counting-on and counting-back strategies. Older children who are working at remembering their math addition facts can use a flip book with numerals on both sides. These children can use mental math strategies to find the sums or have their answers memorized.

- Provide paper, art materials, or rubber stamps, so children can record the combinations they find.

- Challenge children to make a sum different from the target number (with the *Book of 8*, for example, "Can you find two pages that together make ten?").

- Make seasonal versions of the flip books to rekindle interest.

Concepts and Skills Being Learned

- Part-whole relationships.

- Counting on and counting back. Since children have only the first page to work from, they must hunt strategically for matches by envisioning the missing part.

- The commutative property of addition, which states that the order of the numbers being added does not affect the sum. To give an example using the *Book of 8* flip book, one set of matched pages has 3 on the left and 5 on the right, while another has 5 on the left and 3 on the right (3 + 5 and 5 + 3 both equal 8).

ADVICE COLUMN

With activities such as this, the question arises, "How do children know if they got it right?" This is much like the question of whether or not children should have their spelling errors pointed out in their early writing attempts. Children learn from repeated doing, not from having all their errors pointed out to them. Emphasizing getting it right distracts children from giving the best answer they are capable of at the time. Worse yet, having their errors constantly pointed out to them robs the activity of its intrinsic appeal. In fact, if children come up to me and ask, "Is this right?" my response is likely to be something like

- "I don't know. What do you think?"

- "Well, let's look at it. Show me what you did."

- "How can we check?"

- "What do the rest of you think? Explain to them how you did it."

If you want to code materials for self-correction, I advise doing so on the back rather than on the front: use coding dots or matching wallpaper samples on the backs of the matching pages. If you code the pages on the front, either by color, icon, or puzzle cut (that is, the edges of the ones that go together make a perfect fit), children can perform the task without attending to its mathematical aspects.

For most activities, I forego coding the correct answers. When children are operating at the appropriate activity level, they know their answers are right, and catching their own errors is much more gratifying than having their mistakes pointed out to them. If children are making too many errors, it is a signal to me that they are choosing to work at the wrong level. Gently guide them to activities in which they can experience more success.

Closer To

Materials and Setup

☐ Two decks of playing cards, preferably of different designs, each with the face cards removed

Basic Activity

1 Children divide one deck of cards equally among themselves and set the second deck between them.

2 The top card is flipped over on the deck in the center. This provides the target number.

3 Players then flip over the top card on their own pile.

4 The child whose card is closest to the target number wins the trick, and the child takes all the played cards (the target card stays in the center). If two children tie—that is, if both turn over cards that are the same distance from the target number—they play another round to determine the winner.

5 Play continues, with a new target number each time.

6 When the children are out of cards, they pick up the tricks they have won and continue play with those cards. When the target deck is used up, children simply turn the deck over, mix up the cards, and play again.

Extensions and Variations

- Provide manipulatives or art materials for children who need to model or draw the problem.

- Make card decks that have the icons only or the numerals only.

- Change the rules so the child whose card is furthest from the target number wins the trick.

- Provide a giant number line (1 to 10) made from cardboard, an old shower curtain, or a recycled window shade. Each child chooses a number on the number line to stand on (or they spin a spinner, roll a die, etc., to determine where they should stand). One child turns over the target numeral card and places it on the corresponding number on the number line. The child who is standing closest to that number wins a point. If they wish, children can keep score by tallying, using a score sheet, adding a cube to a Unifix stack they hold, or another method.

Concepts and Skills Being Learned

- More, less, and equal.
- The relative size of quantities.
- Counting on and counting back.
- Addition and subtraction facts.

ADVICE COLUMN

Games with moving targets are very powerful in building number sense. Much like being able to find a word in the dictionary, knowing how close one number is to another allows children to move flexibly and strategically in number space. Math curricula that focus prematurely on rote counting skills or on knowing addition and subtraction facts interfere with the development of this nimble number awareness.

I Wish I Had

Materials and Setup

☐ Ten Frame tray or mat (see Ten Frames, pages 61–63)

☐ Ten counters per child

Basic Activity

1 Children take turns making a quantity on their Ten Frame and then announcing, "I have _____."

2 Other children make that quantity on their Ten Frames.

3 The lead child then says, "I wish I had _____" (names another larger or smaller quantity).

4 Without adding or taking away any counters from their frames, the other children advise the lead child how many more counters are needed or how many must be removed to reach the target number. Discussion continues until the children reach consensus or agree to disagree.

5 Children make the new quantity on their Ten Frames and decide whether or not they guessed correctly.

Extensions and Variations

- Children can determine the target number using two 0 to 5 dice, a 1 to 10 spinner, or a deck of cards, ace to 10. (See page 164 for instructions on how to make dice and spinners.)

- Rather than announcing what the new quantity will be, the lead child says, "I wish I had _____ *more*" or "I wish I had _____ *less*." The other children then guess what the new quantity is before moving any counters.

- Do the activity without the Ten Frames—use only the loose counters. This is more difficult since the children can't use the visual patterning around 5 and 10 as an aid.

- Provide each child with two Ten Frames. The children can then extend their numbers above 10.

- To do the activity at a class-wide level, use a transparent Ten Frame on an overhead projector or a large Ten Frame wall chart with Velcro fasteners in the squares and on the counters.

Concepts and Skills Being Learned

- Adding and subtracting quantities relative to 5 and 10.
- Counting on and counting back.

ADVICE COLUMN

The more practice children get in manipulating numbers on the Ten Frame, the more confident they become in their answers. Eventually they make the transition to knowing the answers rather than having to figure them out. In other words, at some point they have memorized their math facts. If we allow children to spend a long time at this mental level, they become much less likely to use their fingers to solve addition and subtraction problems when they reach grade school.

How Many Ways Can You Make It?

for ONE or MORE children

COMMERCIAL PRODUCT

Materials and Setup

☐ Set of 1 to 10 Cuisenaire rods

Design Note: Cuisenaire rods are color-coded, so children can recognize quantities by sight. At the same time, the rods aren't visibly segmented, so children can't count segments to come up with a solution. You can make a comparable set by cutting plastic straws or dowels into lengths from 1 cm to 10 cm and using permanent markers to color-code each length.

Basic Activity

1 Children select a Cuisenaire rod as the target quantity.

2 They then select 2 rods they think equal the target rod when the 2 are added together (see photo below).

3 They check their guesses by putting the 2 rods together next to the target rod, comparing the lengths, and revising their guesses if necessary.

4 Keeping the same target rod, children try to find other combinations of rods that equal the target length.

5 Children look at all the pairs they have made so far and consider whether they might be able to make still more pairs that equal the target quantity.

Extensions and Variations

- Children can look for 3 rods that combine to equal the target rod.
- They can use the 10-rod plus one of the 1- to 9-rods, so the target number will be in the teens. They then need to use multiple smaller rods to equal the above-10 target number.
- They can record their results using Cuisenaire rubber stamps (available from most educational supply companies). For example, if the target is 9, they can stamp a 9-rod on their paper, and then use the 4-rod and 5-rod stamps to record one of their solutions. Alternately, children can use other art materials to draw the Cuisenaire rod solutions, or write down the numerals corresponding to their solutions on sheets of paper.

Concepts and Skills Being Learned

- Part-whole relationships.
- Commutative property of addition. In this activity, it doesn't matter if children add the 3-rod to the 6-rod, or the 6-rod to the 3-rod. Both combinations add up to the 9-rod.
- Counting on and counting back.

ADVICE COLUMN

In the beginning, children may assemble combinations using guess-and-check, much as they would approach any puzzle task. This is acceptable. However, the activity's greatest value occurs when children start to predict what quantities are needed to make the whole instead of discovering solutions through trial and error. You can encourage them to do this by saying things like

- "Here you used a four and a five to make nine. What do you think you'll need to add to the three to make nine?" Once they respond, you can ask them how they know that.
- "Look at the four next to the nine. Do you think the other rod will be longer or shorter than a four? How do you know? What number do you think it will be?"
- "You made seven with a two and a five. What if I took your five away and replaced it with another two—what rod would you need to add to make the seven? How do you know?"
- "Do you know what rod will go with the three to make eight? Okay—put those two rods together and see if you're right."
- "You put a five and a five together, and it was a little too big. What rod do you think you should replace the five with? How do you know that?"

Egg Carton Sum Shaker

for
ONE
or **MORE**
children

Materials and Setup

☐ Egg carton (use one with no holes or gaps in the bottom or top)

☐ Twelve dot stickers with the numerals 0 to 5 written on them (2 stickers for each numeral). Affix each sticker to the bottom of one of the egg carton compartments

☐ Two transparent Bingo chips

Basic Activity

1 Children put the Bingo chips in a carton, close the carton, and shake it vigorously.

2 They open the carton, see which compartments holds Bingo chips, and add up the numerals in those two compartments.

Extensions and Variations

- Children can

  - compare their scores to other children's shakes

  - use their scores to assemble a 1 to 10 Cuisenaire or Unifix staircase—they need to shake each sum before they can add it to the staircase, and the first child to complete a staircase wins

  - keep a running tally of each sum on a recording sheet

  - figure out the difference between the two quantities rather than their sum

- Make the shaker with half the stickers showing numerals and the other half showing 0 to 5 dots.

- Put three Bingo chips in the shaker so that they either have to add all three, or add two numbers and subtract the third.

- Make this a group game where the child with the largest sum wins points during each round. Points are equal to the difference between the child's sum and the next highest sum.

Concepts and Skills Being Learned

- Part-whole relationships.

- Counting on and counting back.

- The relative size of quantities.

- Addition and subtraction facts.

ADVICE COLUMN

Some children are more willing to engage in this mental exercise if you embed it in a game or a social context. Call it competitive, if you wish. The children call it fun.

Only children who are fairly advanced in their number sense should be doing tasks in which they must know the number fact in order to succeed. Manipulatives should always be available for those children who need to model the solution physically.

Balance-Scale Problems

Materials and Setup

☐ Mechanical balance scale

☐ Manipulatives that are somewhat heavy and of uniform weight (for example, large washers or 2-inch floor tiles. The addition of a single manipulative should make a distinct difference in tipping the scale)

Design Note: I have made perfectly suitable balance scales by hanging buckets from the ends of a broom handle, and then suspending the middle of the broom handle from the ceiling, using a bracket for hanging plants. Even something as simple as small baskets hanging from the ends of a large plastic clothes hanger can work.

Basic Activity

1 The first child places a number of tiles on one side of the scale and announces the quantity: "I am putting six tiles on this side."

2 The same child places a different quantity of tiles on the other side of the scale and announces the quantity: "I am putting four tiles on this side."

3 The first child asks, "Where should I put more tiles to make the scale balance? How many tiles should I add?"

4 The second child then suggests an amount.

5 The first child follows the second child's directions, and together they see if the solution brings the scale into balance.

Extensions and Variations

- The first child asks how many tiles should be removed from one side or the other to make the scale balance.

- The first child adds a quantity to the first side, a quantity to the second, an additional quantity to the first, and then asks the second child how many tiles need to be added (or subtracted) to make the scale balance.

- The first child adds quantities to the first side of the scale in sets (for example, in sets of two—"I'm putting in two . . . and two more . . . and two more. How many should I add to the other side to make it balance?").

Concepts and Skills Being Learned

- Part-whole relationships.

- Counting on and counting back.

- Adding and subtracting quantities.

- Skip counting (that is, adding quantities to the scale two or more at a time. This new way of counting is the beginning point for understanding multiplication).

ADVICE COLUMN

What greater proof that a math equation is balanced than by leveling the pans of a balance scale? This is a great way to explore number sense using a piece of equipment normally associated with science. It is always worthwhile to show children new uses for familiar materials.

Pattern Block Addition

for
ONE
or **MORE**
children

COMMERCIAL
PRODUCT

Materials and Setup

☐ Pattern blocks. Plastic versions of these blocks are not expensive and are available from most educational supply companies. A template for a set of tagboard pattern blocks appears on page 208. If you're using a commercial set, remove the orange squares and the tan rhombi. Using the geometric relationships within the set, make a chart showing the following block values:

- 1 green equilateral triangle = 1
- 1 blue rhombus = 2 (it takes 2 green equilateral triangles to make the rhombus)
- 1 red trapezoid = 3 (it takes 3 green equilateral triangles to make the trapezoid)
- 1 yellow hexagon = 6 (it takes 6 green equilateral triangles to make the hexagon)

Note: Templates for the pattern blocks can also be found online at www .teachervision.com.

Basic Activity

1 Children create a design or image using the pattern blocks.

2 They compute how much their designs are worth by figuring out how many green equilateral triangles are needed to make the same design. Most children do this either by placing green equilateral triangles over the original design or, once they have more experience with this activity, by using the values listed above.

Extensions and Variations

- Provide counters so children can count out 6 counters for each hexagon in their design, 3 counters for each trapezoid, etc. They can then count the pile of counters to determine their design's total value.

- Set a target number. Children then try to make as many designs as possible that equal that number of green triangles.

- The class can use rubber pattern block stamps (available from most educational supply companies) to create different patterns that add up to the same quantity. Children can then collect these designs and make a class book, such as *Our Book of 6*. If they wish, they can write the equivalent numerals inside each of the stamped pattern block outlines. They can then put the book in the classroom library.

- Children can also use the rubber pattern block stamps to make pattern block designs of their choosing. They write down the values of the individual pieces and of the total design. For example, they might make a person using 2 yellow hexagons stamps for the head and body and 4 blue rhombi stamps for the limbs, writing the numeral 6 inside each of the hexagons, the numeral 2 inside each of the rhombi, and the numeral 20 on the page to indicate the design's value.

- Children create a pattern block design that has the same quantity as the number of letters in their names. For example, a child named Jeremy, who has six letters in his name, might use two red trapezoids (3 + 3 = 6) or make a blue rhombus/green triangle/blue rhombus/green triangle pattern (2 + 1 + 2 + 1 = 6).

Concepts and Skills Being Learned

- Part-whole relationships.

- Counting on.

- Skip counting (for example, counting the red trapezoids as "Three, six, nine.")

ADVICE COLUMN

Children need lots of opportunities to use the pattern blocks in other contexts to develop an intuitive sense of how many pieces of one kind are needed to make another piece. Consider putting the pattern blocks in the puzzle or the block construction area.

In the math curriculum, many exercises use geometric relationships to make mathematical relationships visible. These are ideally suited to young children who are still very rooted in the concrete world.

The Literature Connection

ADVICE COLUMN

Seeing the same number split up in different ways is one of the most important new frontiers in young children's evolving number sense. Unhappily, I have found few books for young children that focus on this aspect of number sense. Aspiring authors, take note.

Bogart, Jo Ellen. 1989. *10 for Dinner*. New York: Scholastic.

Jenkins, Emily. 2001. *Five Creatures*. New York: Farrar, Straus and Giroux.

Merriam, Eve. 1996. *12 Ways to Get to 11*. New York: Aladdin/Simon & Schuster.

7
counting higher

In some ways, counting higher is simply a matter of learning more number names and getting good at reciting them in the proper order. The transition points between decades are problematic for a while ("What comes after twenty-nine?"), especially when children try to count backward ("What comes before thirty?").

Children love to show off how high they can count, but that's not enough. We need to give them activities in which they have to actually count large quantities, not just rattle off numbers out loud. Chapter 7 offers some suggestions for activities that encourage them to play around with larger numbers. You know children are ready for activities in this chapter if

- they show an interest in bigger numbers

- they like to show off how high they can count

- they spontaneously read numerals in the teens, twenties, or beyond (for example, numerals on the calendar or on a hundreds board)

- they understand the pattern of how numbers 1 to 9 repeat after decade points (" . . . thirty-eight, thirty-nine, forty. Forty-one, forty-two . . .")

- they can answer questions about relative quantity in larger numbers (for example, when you take classroom attendance, you might ask, "We normally have 23 children in our class, but only 21 are here today. So how many of our friends are missing?")

We also want to help children develop a sense of how big those big numbers really are. In other words, we want them to start estimating. What does 20 of something look like? How about 50 of something? If you put 25 pennies in a basket and say, "Wow, there certainly are a lot of pennies in this basket. About how many do you think there are?" Children should be able to make reasonable guesses like 20, 30, or even 40, not 8, 100, or a million. Children need lots of opportunities to guess how many are in a set and then to count how many are actually there so that number names and numerals start to have real meaning.

And don't neglect to ask the follow-up questions: "So you guessed forty pennies, and there were actually twenty-five. Did you guess too high or too low?" Children are confident that 7 is more than 5, but they have less experience with numbers like 25 and 40. It takes some time before they become confident about which is larger, but now is a good time for them to start pondering those questions and devising strategies for figuring out the answers.

Piggy Bank

Materials and Setup

☐ Children's piggy bank, with an easily removable bottom

☐ Basket with 100 pennies

Basic Activity

1 Children count pennies one by one as they drop them into the piggy bank's slot.

Extensions and Variations

- Provide a penny rubber stamp (available from most educational supply companies). The child stamps 100 pennies on a piece of paper. Of course, it need not be a penny stamp. The child can get the same practice by stamping any image 100 times.

- The child counts by 2s, dropping 2 pennies at a time into the slot.

- Provide 10 dimes and a $1 bill. As the child reaches each decade in the count, she places a dime on the table in front of the piggy bank. Once all 100 pennies are in the bank, the child counts the dimes, skip counting by 10s. When she reaches the last dime, rather than saying "one hundred," she says, "One dollar," and pulls out the $1 bill.

- Have the children take turns adding the pennies to the piggy bank and saying the next number. This is actually quite difficult for children. They have a hard time picking up someone else's count.

- For less advanced counters, children count repeatedly to a given number (say, 5 or 10) while putting the pennies in the bank ("One, two, three, four, five. One, two, three, four, five. One, two . . .").

- For more advanced counters,

  - children count backward, starting with 100 as they put the first penny in the slot. As they put the last penny in the bank, they say, "One," then "Zero," as they point proudly to the empty basket.

  - once children have counted all 100 pennies and placed them in the bank, hand them a second set of 100 pennies and let them keep going.

Concepts and Skills Being Learned

- Counting on. Children are forced to pause after each number because of the intervening fine-motor task of getting the penny into the slot. This breaks up the rhythm of simply rattling off the numbers and forces the children to think about what number they just said and what number comes after that.

- Counting through the decades ("After thirty-nine comes what?"). Many children may slip into saying, "Thirty-ten, thirty-eleven, thirty twelve" before catching themselves.

- Coin values.

- Skip counting.

ADVICE COLUMN

This is such a simple activity, and children love it. There is something mesmerizing about the rhythm of picking up pennies and dropping them in the slot.

Don't rush in to rescue a child whose count is off because he loses his place, repeats a decade, or misses the decade switches ("forty ten, forty eleven, forty twelve . . ."). Once he realizes something is wrong, let *him* decide how to recover.

If a child complains that there weren't 100 pennies after he's put all of them in the bank, ask him to count the set one more time. Unlike an adult, he won't be upset by this request. If he still comes up with a number other than 100, have him put the pennies in piles of 10 and count by 10s. If the count is truly off, ask the child how many pennies he should add or subtract to make it exactly 100 and then give him that many pennies to add to the bank or ask him to take that many out. He'll be so proud that he has fixed the set, and you'll be happy that he got in so much valuable counting practice.

Toothpick Shaker Estimation

for **TWO** *or* **MORE** *children*

Materials and Setup

☐ Clear plastic shaker bottle with holes in the top (The containers used in restaurants for grated cheese or hot peppers work well. Any container with holes punched in the top works, so be creative.)

☐ Flat toothpicks (If children are too young to use toothpicks safely, they can use other materials such as coffee stirrers, but you'll also need to provide a container with larger holes in the lid.)

☐ Number line (optional)

Basic Activity

1 One child puts the toothpicks in the shaker bottle, screws on the lid, and asks, "If I turn this bottle upside down and shake it 3 times, how many toothpicks do you think will fall out?"

2 The other children make their guesses. The first child then turns the bottle over, shakes it vigorously up, and then down, exactly 3 times, and turns it back upright again. (Most often the number of toothpicks that fall out will be somewhere between 20 and 30.)

3 Before counting the toothpicks that fell out, the first child asks the other children if they think their guesses were pretty close or if they guessed too high or too low.

4 After the children respond, the first child counts the toothpicks one by one while the group counts along out loud.

5 The children then discuss the results relative to their guesses.

6 Either the same or a different child puts the toothpicks back in the bottle and repeats the activity.

Extensions and Variations

- Children don't replace the toothpicks after each trial. They find it interesting that the number of toothpicks that fall out becomes smaller and smaller as the trials progress. This provides another prediction they can make: "How many times do we need to shake the container before it's empty?"

- Children can count the toothpicks by 2s.

- Ask a follow-up question: "You guessed ____, and ____ actually fell out. How many more/fewer would have had to fall out for your guess to be right?"

- For younger children, put just 10 toothpicks in the bottle.
- For older children, put 10 or 20 toothpicks in the bottle. After the children have counted how many toothpicks fell out, let them estimate how many toothpicks are still in the bottle. Then they open the container, remove the rest of the toothpicks, and count them.

Concepts and Skills Being Learned

- Becoming comfortable with estimating. Children tend to believe that any guess that is not exact is wrong. However, if the actual amount is close to what they estimated, they did it right.

- The relative size of numbers beyond 10. Children may have a hard time comparing their guesses to the actual number of toothpicks because they have less practice involving numbers higher than 10. That's when a number line can be useful. Children can use the distance between the numerals on the line as a guide for evaluating how close the numbers are to each other.

- Probability. Having seen how many toothpicks fell out the first few times, children have seen a range of the possible results, so they can make better estimates of how many might fall out. However, most children still have a hard time understanding that no amount of practice allows them to be absolutely certain how many will fall out on the next trial.

- Control of variables. If the experiment is not done the same way each time, it is not fair. For example, if the child shakes the container vigorously one time and gently the next, it affects the results.

ADVICE COLUMN

You'd be surprised how many children are expert counters but lousy estimators. Looking at a quantity and estimating how many there are is a separate skill from being able to count accurately. The number 20 is the most common estimate of quantities that look like a lot to young children. Developing a sense of what about 20 looks like (versus about 30, about 50, and about 100) is an essential skill for children to develop as they start counting bigger numbers.

Handfuls Game II

Materials and Setup

☐ Container full of small objects. A mixed group of objects is fine, and providing objects of different sizes adds an interesting twist to the game

☐ More/Less spinner (See page 164 for information on making your own spinner and page 210 for a template.)

Basic Activity

1 Each child grabs a handful of objects.

2 Children count their collections and compare amounts.

3 They spin the More/Less spinner to decide who wins this round. If they spin *More*, the child with the most objects wins, and if they spin *Less*, the child with the least number of objects wins.

4 After each round, they put the objects back in the box and play again.

Extensions and Variations

- Children cluster their objects in groups of 10 to verify amounts (say, 4 piles of 10 and 5 more make 45).

  - For children who can read larger numerals, provide a number line to help the children decide whose amount is larger. Young children have limited experience reading 2-digit numerals or learning about the 10s place and the 1s place, so they may frequently confuse numerals like 23 and 32.

  - For more mature counters, children spin the More/Less spinner to decide who must change his quantity to equal that of his partner (if they spin *More*, the child with more objects must return some to the box so that she has an equal amount to that of her partner). Accomplishing this task is an interesting challenge for children.

Concepts and Skills Being Learned

- Relative size of larger quantities.
- Reading larger numerals.

ADVICE COLUMN

Deciding who has more is very difficult for young children, even when they can successfully count quantities over 10. Just looking at the piles doesn't give them much information, either. They have to know which of the counts represents a larger quantity. Until they have a better sense of place value, it remains difficult for them to decide if 28 or 32 is a bigger number. Providing a number line helps make this task more manageable and fosters interesting conversations.

What's Missing? Number Charts

for ONE or MORE children

Materials and Setup

☐ Number charts in various configurations (for example, 4 x 5, 5 x 5, 6 x 4, 5 x 7)

☐ 1 inch x 1 inch counting tiles with numerals written on them. You can also make these out of tagboard cut into 1 inch squares

Note: Fill in the number charts with consecutive numerals left to right and top to bottom, starting with 1, but leave some of the numeral spaces blank. Write the numerals corresponding to these blank spaces on the tiles.

Basic Activity

1 Children place the tiles on the chart in their proper numerical order.

Extensions and Variations

• Challenge children to start with the tiles face down and try to place each tile they turn over on the chart before they choose new tiles. This forces them to figure out where to put the tiles using the numeral cues already on the board (for example, "There's the fifteen and sixteen, so seventeen would go here,") and not just start at the 1 square on the chart and work upward.

• Provide a number line for the children to use as a guide to help determine which numerals go where.

• Provide a chart that doesn't start at 1.

• Provide a chart that counts by 2s.

• Children can play a more/less game using only the tiles. Start with all the tiles face down. Each child chooses a tile. The child who has more/less takes the trick.

• For children who can write their numerals, provide a Missing Numeral chart made of erasable material so children can write the missing numerals in the blank spaces.

Concepts and Skills Being Learned

• Counting larger numbers and reading larger numerals.

• Numerical order.

• Relative size of numbers.

ADVICE COLUMN

You may want to color-code the numeral tiles to their respective charts, since sets of tiles often get mixed up by accident.

Avoid making the charts 10 columns wide. In this activity, encourage children to find the proper place for a tile using something other than visual patterning—not just putting the 24 on the row with the 20s and in the column where all the units are 4. Even using a number line to check their work proves challenging for young children, since one chart has numerals in a straight line and the other chart has numerals arranged left-to-right and top-to-bottom.

Watch *how* children fill in their charts. Less mature counters start with 1 and work forward. More mature counters confidently pick up any tile and know where it goes relative to the other numerals on the chart.

The Literature Connection

COMMERCIAL
PRODUCT

ADVICE COLUMN

Children who can count past 10 are usually eager to show off their abilities. Books that allow them to experiment with counting large quantities are a good way for them to flex their new-found math muscles. The small size and complex arrangements of the pictured objects require good eye-hand coordination. The scattered arrangement of the pictured objects also encourages children not to miss anything or count anything twice—instead, they must practice counting in an organized way.

Counting by 1s Past 10

Beaton, Clare. 1999. *One Moose, Twenty Mice.* Cambridge, Mass.: Barefoot Books.

Carlstrom, Nancy W. 1996. *Let's Count It Out, Jesse Bear.* New York: Simon & Schuster.

Cleveland, David. 1978. *The April Rabbits.* New York: Coward, McCann & Geoghegan.

Disney. 2000. *My Very First Disney 1-2-3 Counting Book.* New York: Disney Children's Books.

Mazzola, Frank Jr. 1997. *Counting Is for the Birds.* Watertown, Mass.: Charlesbridge.

McGrath, Barbara B. 1999. *The Baseball Counting Book.* Watertown, Mass.: Charlesbridge.

Rankin, Laura. 1998. *The Handmade Counting Book.* New York: Penguin.

Ryan, Pam M., and Jerry Pallotta. 1996. *The Crayon Counting Book.* Watertown, Mass.: Charlesbridge.

Counting By 10s Past 10

Fleming, Denise. 1992. *Count.* New York: Henry Holt.

Miranda, Anne. 1999. *Monster Math.* Orlando, Fla.: Harcourt Brace.

Sloat, Teri. 1991. *From One to One Hundred.* New York: Scholastic.

8

miscellaneous games

In this chapter, you'll find many board games, homemade and commercial, and card games that can augment your math curriculum. You'll also find a sampling of math games from other parts of the world.

Board Games

Materials and Setup

☐ Homemade game boards (These can be made from laminated tagboard or cardboard, donated pizza boxes, etc. See page 165 for specific design specifications.)

☐ Game pieces for each player (The pieces should be unique for each player. They are used for moving on the board and marking squares that have been captured. Buttons, translucent Bingo chips, erasers, and other small manipulatives work well.)

☐ Probability generator (This is a fancy way of describing spinners, dice, or playing cards that can be used to decide how many spaces to move and who takes the first turn. To simplify things, I use the term *spinner*.)

Making Spinners

Note: Templates for spinners can be found on pages 210–211; blank spinners can also be purchased through most educational supply catalogs.

1 To make a spinner, you will need tagboard, a wire brad, and a small metal washer from the hardware store.

2 Photocopy the spinner template and paste it smoothly onto a piece of tagboard.

3 With a marker, label the different sections of the spinner. For example, if you are making a spinner as a replacement for a die, you can label the 6 sections with numbers or with pictured quantities.

4 Photocopy the arrow from page 210–211, paste it onto tagboard, and cut it out after it has dried. Drill or punch a smooth hole through the center of the arrow.

5 Place the brad through the arrow, through the metal washer, and then through the base of the spinner. Fold the ends of the brad down on the back of the base and tape the ends in place. Lift the head of the brad up a bit so the arrow turns freely. You're done. The washer keeps the arrow from rubbing on the surface of the base while it spins. If the spinner binds up, lift the head of the brad or flatten the base and you've solved the problem.

Making Dice

Note: Blank dice can be purchased in most educational supply catalogs; a template for making a die appears on page 212. Simply photocopy the template, paste it to a piece of cardboard, cut it out, and assemble as directed. Use a permanent marker to write or draw on the different faces of the cube, or attach small stickers to signify different quantities.

Blank cubes of any size can be turned into dice. Make sure that they are truly cube-shaped, though. Otherwise your dice will be rigged. Scrap wood can be made into serviceable cubes using a table saw. Children also enjoy using large Styrofoam or foam cubes as dice.

Activities

Quantity Match or Quantity-Numeral Match

1. Make a game board containing 20 to 30 squares in any configuration (4 x 5, 4 x 6, 5 x 6, etc.). On each of the squares, draw a pictured quantity, 1 through 6. Vary the pictures and their patterned arrangements.

2. For Quantity Match, create a spinner showing the same quantities as the game board. For Quantity-Numeral Match, make a spinner with numerals instead.

3. Give each player 20 to 30 game pieces of the same color. Each player needs a different color.

4. Players take turns spinning the spinner and finding a matching square to mark with their game piece. Children cannot place their game pieces on a square that is already covered by another game piece. If no match can be made, those children skip their turns.

5. Play continues until all the squares are covered. The player with the most tokens on the board at the end of the game wins.

One More or One Less

One More and One Less are played the same way as Quantity Match or Quantity-Numeral Match, except children must cover a square on the board that contains one more (or one less) than the quantity or numeral shown on the spinner.

Racetrack

1. Create a game board modeled on a racetrack. There should be a start line and a finish line and 3 or 4 lanes in which the children's game pieces race. Divide each lane into a series of approximately 20 squares. (See also Race to 20, pages 42–43.)

2. Create a spinner (see template on page 211) with 6 equal sections. Three of the sections should show the numerals 1 through 3. The other 3 sections should show the same numerals but with circles around them. This second set represents negative quantities (in other words, children must move their game pieces backward that number of spaces).

3. Children take turns spinning the spinner and moving toward (or away from) the finish line. The game ends when all the children have reached the finish line.

Worm Hunt

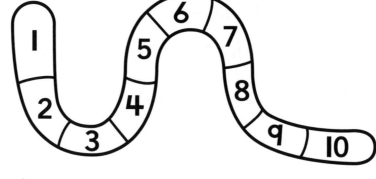

1. Create a spinner that contains the numerals 1 to 10.

2. Create a set of worms. Use the template for worms on page 209. Photocopy the template and color each worm a different color, using crayons or markers.
Glue the worms to tagboard or cardboard, and then cut out each worm. Then cut each of the worms into 10 segments.

3. Play starts with all the worm pieces set randomly in the middle. Players choose which color worm they are going to build. Players take turns spinning the spinner, collecting the corresponding segments of their worms, and adding them to their worms in correct position. The first child to assemble all ten pieces of her worm in numerical order wins. Children can play until all the worms have been assembled.

ADVICE COLUMN

You may want to create more than one version of some of these game boards, such as the one described in Quantity Match or Quantity-Numeral Match. Doing so keeps children from memorizing what answers go where and allows you to introduce seasonal or thematic variations.

Card Games

Materials and Setup

☐ One or more decks of playing cards

Activities

Pick a Pair

1. This game is played with a deck of 40 cards, ace through 10. The ace is treated as a 1.

2. The first player turns over 6 cards from the deck. If she sees a match, she takes that pair and adds 2 more cards from the deck to the display. Her turn continues until she can make no more matches. Leftover cards are inserted back into the deck at random points, and the next player takes his turn.

3. Play continues until the deck is gone. The child with the most pairs wins.

We're Number One

1. This game is played with a pair of dice and a deck of 48 cards, ace through queen. In this game, the ace represents 1, the jack represents 11, and the queen represents 12.

2. Each player chooses a suit. Children divide up the cards so that each one has all of the cards in a suit. They then lay out the cards in numerical order.

3. Players take turns rolling the 2 dice and removing the card from their set that matches the rolled sum. The first child left with only an ace wins the round. (The ace remains because it's impossible to roll a 1 die using 2 dice.)

4. For an alternative, use 1 die with dots and 1 die with numerals 1 through 6.

Five in a Row

1. This game is played with a deck of 40 cards, ace through 10. The ace represents 1.

2. Each child starts with 5 cards. Children take turns drawing a card from the deck and choosing a card to discard. Play continues until one child has 5 consecutive numbers in his hand.

Going on a Pair Hunt

1 This game is played with a pair of dice and a full deck of 52 cards.

2 Begin with all of the cards in the draw pile. Children take turns rolling the two dice and taking that many cards from the deck. They then make whatever pairs they can from the drawn cards and put the rest in the discard pile.

3 After the draw pile is gone, children reshuffle the discard pile to use it as the new draw pile. Play continues until all of the cards have been paired.

Blast Off

1 This game is played with a deck of 42 cards, ace through 10, plus the 2 jokers. The ace represents 1.

2 The game begins with all of the cards in the draw pile. Children take turns drawing cards, one card per turn. If a child draws a 10, she keeps it; otherwise, she discards the card. After she gets a 10, she next searches for a 9, and then an 8, etc.

3 When the draw pile is gone, the discard pile is reshuffled and used as the new draw pile. Play continues until a child who already has the cards 10 to 1 draws a joker, at which point he yells, "Blast Off!"

Crazy Eights

1 This game is played with a full deck of 52 cards.

2 To start the game, each player is dealt 6 cards. The remaining cards are placed face down in the center, and the top card is flipped over to start the discard pile.

3 The first child looks at the cards in her hand and tries to make a match with the card on top of the discard pile, either in number or suit. If she has a match, she places it on top of the discard pile. If she does not have a match, she draws more cards from the deck until she can make a match. Eights can be played at any time and allow the child to name the suit to be played next.

4 The children take turns trying to get rid of the cards in their hands by matching either the number or the suit of the last card played. This either/or quality makes it very challenging for young children. Play ends when one child has managed to discard all of her cards.

Snap Variations

1 This game is played with a homemade deck of 40 cards, 1 through 10. Half of the cards have dots to represent their quantity and the other half have numerals.

2 One child deals all the cards to the players. Two players simultaneously turn over their top card (they may need to chant "One, two, three, go," to get synchronized). If the cards are equal, the first child to say "Snap!" takes the trick. The players may need a third child to act as a referee and decide which child said "Snap!" first. If the cards are not equal, the children continue to turn over cards until an equal match is made, and the child who says "snap!" first takes the two piles of played cards. If a child says "Snap!" and the cards are not equal, his opponent takes the trick.

Extensions and Variations

- The children say "Snap!" if the numbers on their cards are one apart.
- One child rolls a die, another turns over a card from a deck that only goes up to 6. If the 2 are equal, the first child to say "Snap!" takes the card. If they use a 10-faced die or a 1 to 10 spinner, the numbers on the deck can go up to ten. Children can also use a die or cards that show numerals rather than quantities.

ADVICE COLUMN

In most cases, these card games can be played with regular playing cards, or you can make specialty decks, such as

- decks showing only numerals
- decks showing pictured quantities
- decks showing pictured quantities in non-patterned arrangements
- decks with some quantity cards and some numeral cards

Young children may have a hard time holding playing cards in their hands. This is even more difficult if they simultaneously need to look at the quantities on the card, not just the numerals in the corners. You might want to provide them with card holders or card shields that allow them to view their cards comfortably without their opponents seeing them.

Games from Around the World

Materials and Setup

Vary by game

Activities

Mancala (African and Asian)

This game is played around the world and also goes by the names Kalah, Wari, Oware, Sungka, and Bao. Mancala (from the Arabic, meaning *transferring*) and its variants are probably the most played board games on the planet, in part because they need only indentations dug into the earth and a few small stones or seeds to play. The board for playing has 2 rows of 6 (sometimes 4) wells, with a larger well (the mancalas) at both ends. I have made a mancala board out of materials as simple as an egg carton with bowls placed at each end (see illustration).

1 The object of the game is to try to capture and store as many stones as possible in your mancala.

2 Each player chooses a row and a mancala to play. Play starts with 4 stones in each of the 12 wells.

3 A turn consists of a player taking all the stones from one of her wells and distributing them one at a time in a clockwise direction in the wells and in her mancala (skipping over her opponent's mancala).

4 Two important rules make this a game of strategy, not of luck:

- if a player's last stone lands in her mancala, she gets another turn
- if a player's last stone lands in an empty well on her side, she takes that stone and all of the stones in her opponent's well directly opposite the one she landed in and puts them in her mancala

5 Players don't have individual game pieces—rather, they play with whatever stones are on their side.

6 The game ends when one player empties all of her wells. When this happens, the player takes all of the stones remaining in her opponent's wells and adds them to her mancala before the final count. The player with the most stones in her mancala wins.

Dreidel (Hebrew)

This game uses the four-sided spinning top commonly used by Jewish children around Hanukkah. Each side of the top shows a different symbol—*nun*, *gimel*, *he*, and *shin*, which are the first letters of each word in the Hebrew phrase *Nes gadol hayah sham*, meaning "A great miracle happened here." A template for making a flat version of dreidel appears on page 213, which you can photocopy, glue to cardboard, and cut out. Puncture a small hole in the center of the dreidel and push a sharpened pencil through the hole. The dreidel will spin on the pencil's point. You can also purchase dreidels at most educational or toy stores.

1 In the dreidel game, players all start with ten counters, two of which they place in the pot. Players take turns spinning the dreidel. The dreidel symbol that lands on top tells the player what action to take.

- *nun* (0)—That is, do nothing.
- *gimel*—Take all of the counters in the pot. Each player then adds two more counters to the pot before play continues.
- *hey*—Take half the pot. If there are an odd number of counters in the pot, the player takes the leftover one as well.
- *shin*—Add two counters to the pot.

2 Play ends when one child runs out of counters. The child with the most counters wins.

Toma-Todo (Mexican)

The game Toma-Todo, which means *Take All*, comes from Mexico and is similar to the dreidel game, except that children use a 6-sided top. A template for making the top appears on page 214. You can also write the following 6 phrases on the faces of a large die or use a spinner

- *Toma uno* (Take one)
- *Toma dos* (Take two)
- *Toma todo* (Take all)
- *Pon uno* (Put one)
- *Pon dos* (Put two)
- *Todos ponen* (All put—all players put two counters into the pot)

The rules are otherwise the same as in the dreidel game.

Patolli (Aztec)

From the Aztecs, we get a game that's a simplified version of Parcheesi. The board's path is in an x-pattern, with the arms 4 squares long and 2 squares wide. A reproducible Patolli board appears on page 215, which you can photocopy, cut out, and glue to tagboard.

1 Each player starts out with 6 game pieces at start boxes on opposite ends of the board.

2 Five lima beans, each with a dot on one side, are used to determine the number of spaces a player can move one piece in a counterclockwise direction. After throwing the lima beans, the number of dots showing indicates the number of spaces to move. If the player rolls a 5, she doubles it and moves 10 spaces. Players cannot land on a space occupied by an opponent's piece. They must either move a different piece or skip their turn.

3 The first player to get all 6 pieces back to the start box wins.

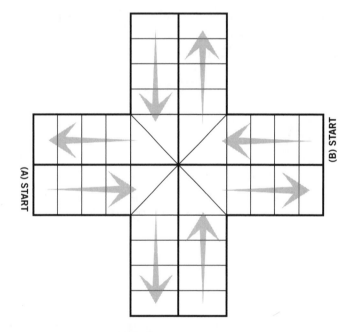

Lu-Lu (Hawaiian)

Lu-Lu (meaning *to shake*) is traditionally played with 4 flat stones. Children can substitute plastic discs or large lima beans. The stones are marked on one side with 1, 2, 3, or 4 dots. The other side of the stones is blank. The game can be played with a single set of stones, but for young children it is better if all players have their own set. This way, they don't have to wait their turn.

To play, the children toss their stones and score the number of dots showing. The player with the most dots on the toss wins.

Kawasusuts (Native American; tribe unknown)

This path game is played on a circular board with gates or starting spaces (called *Siammi*) located in the north, south, east, and west quadrants of the board, with 10 path spaces marked along the outer rim between the Siammi. A reproducible game board appears on page 216, which you can photocopy, cut out, and glue to tagboard or cardboard.

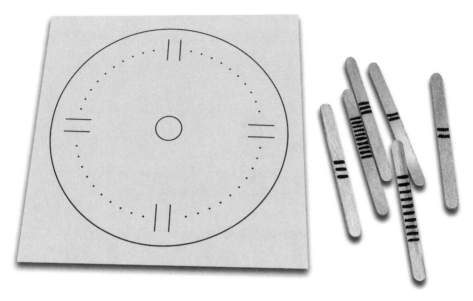

1. Each player begins on one of the Siammis. To move, a player tosses three craft sticks (one marked with 2 stripes on both sides, one with 3 stripes, and one with 10 stripes) and moves that number of stripes along the path.

2. Landing in another gate or having an opponent land on your piece's space bumps you back to your Siammi.

3. The first player to complete a lap of the board wins the round.

ADVICE COLUMN

A host of traditional playground games and songs teach mathematical principles, many with historical or cultural significance. Children throughout history and around the world have enjoyed challenging themselves logically and mathematically, usually with little or no equipment involved. Thanks to Harcourt Brace's *Multicultural Projects: Mathematics from Around the World* (1993), a wonderful collection of some of the games described in this section.

Miscellaneous Activity Formats

Materials and Setup

Vary by game

• •

Activities

Beanbag or Ringtoss Variations

You can add a large-motor component to just about any game by tossing beanbags at targets or tossing rings on pegs. For example, the game's goal can be to

- hit numerals in sequence
- hit a matching numeral and quantity in 2 throws
- hit the highest numeral or quantity
- hit quantities or numerals that are one number apart in 2 throws
- hit the highest sum in 2 or more throws
- hit the total quantity that is closest to 10 in 2 throws

You can make targets using markers or paint on large pieces of durable cardboard. Draw numerals or quantities randomly on the board, spaced widely enough that they make good targets. Adjust their size and distance from where the toss is made to match the physical skills of the children.

Hopscotch Twister

For this game, create a 1 to 10 spinner and a traditional hopscotch outline. To make the hopscotch board indoors, simply use masking or electrical tape on the floor of your classroom. You can also make a portable version using masking tape on a plastic tarp. If it's nice outside, you can make a hopscotch board using chalk on the sidewalk in your outdoor play area.

1. Children spin the spinner and try to move to the space indicated by the spinner in as few steps or hops as possible. In this version, they may also go backward—for example, if a child spins a 4 after spinning a 6, he goes back 2 spaces.

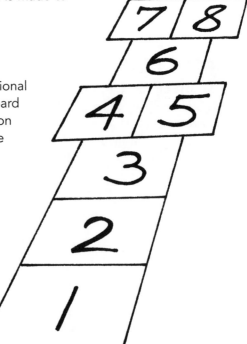

2 Alternatively, the spinner can tell a child how may steps or hops to take (if the child is on the 3 and spins a 2, she hops to the 5). Putting multiple players on the board is another way to make the game interesting.

Blizzard

1 Put two colored dot stickers on 6 clear plastic cups (one at the bottom of each cup and one on the side). Label each pair of stickers with the numerals 1, 2, or 3. There should be 2 cups for each numeral.

2 Cluster the cups randomly on the floor. From chest level, a child sprinkles 10 Styrofoam peanuts from a bowl into the cups.

3 After the peanuts have landed, the child looks to see how many peanuts landed in each of the cups. Each peanut that lands in a cup is worth the number of points written on the cup (for example, if 3 peanuts land in the 2 cup, the child gets 6 points). **Note:** Children may need to be supplied with counters in order to add up their total scores.

ADVICE COLUMN

Young children are developing physically and mentally. Find something that challenges them on both of these levels and you've almost certainly got a hit on your hands. You're only limited by your imagination.

Commercial Games

COMMERCIAL
PRODUCT

Materials and Setup

Vary by game

• •

Activities

Hi Ho! Cherry-O

Western Publishing Company, www.hasbro.com/miltonbradley

The game board has four cherry trees with ten removable cherries on each tree. Each player has a cherry-picking basket and the goal is to pick all ten cherries from your tree. A spinner determines how many cherries to pick, how many to put back on the tree, if a bird or dog eats some, or if the entire basket spills.

Chutes and Ladders

Milton Bradley, www.hasbro.com/miltonbradley

This is a path game that uses numerals from 1 to 100, with ladders for jumping ahead and chutes for sliding backward. **Note:** The path zigzags around, so children who cannot read numerals may need directional arrows added to the board to help them keep track of which way is forward.

Number Neighbors

Old Fashioned Products, www.mugginsmath.com

This game uses large marbles and plastic dimpled marble holders. It's a three-dimensional version of the Parts-of Puzzle Cards activity described on pages 134–135.

STEP 1–25 Board

Insta-Learn, www.insta-learn.com

The Insta-Learn Company puts out a series of sensory, language, and math boards that are great hands-on learning manipulatives. The math board has 25 spaces with pictured dots from 0 to 25 and numeral pieces that fit into the corresponding spaces like puzzle pieces. The game also includes basic problem sets for early learners, with built-in mechanisms for self-checking answers. The beginning problem sets focus on counting quantities and adding and subtracting small quantities, and include fill-in-the-missing-numeral strips.

Mathematics Pentathlon, Division I

Pentathlon Institute, www.mathpentath.org

Mathematics Pentathlon is a series of competitive-cooperative math games in which teams play against one another. Some of the games in division I provide good practice in developing early number sense. For example, Star Track requires players to draw paper clip chains from a bowl (chains are from 2 to 9 links long) to determine their moves on the game board.

ADVICE COLUMN

A host of educational games and software options exist. Beware of those that are attractively disguised drills, such as computer games that present a written addition problem that children must answer correctly before the game rewards them with something interesting on screen. Instead, look for programs that involve real mathematical problem solving embedded in interesting contexts. A good example of software that meets these criteria is *Thinkin' Things Collection 1* (Edmark, www.riverdeep.net).

appendix:
reproducibles

More, Less, Same Labels

Less

Same

More

Color-Quantity Bingo Card

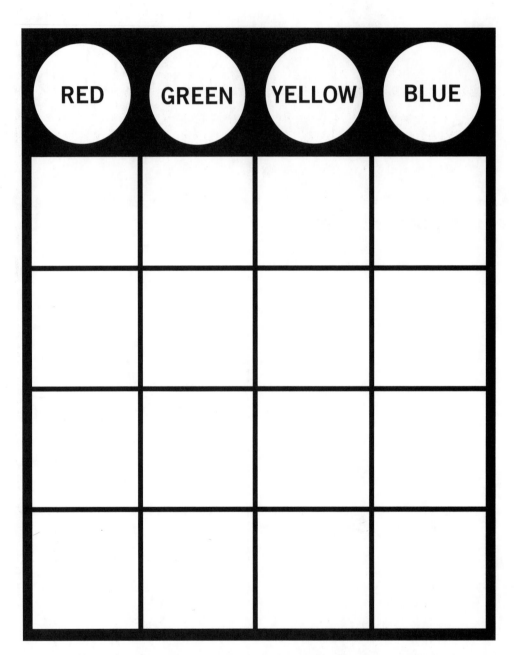

RED   GREEN   YELLOW   BLUE

(Circles should be colored with appropriate colors)

Racetrack Game Board

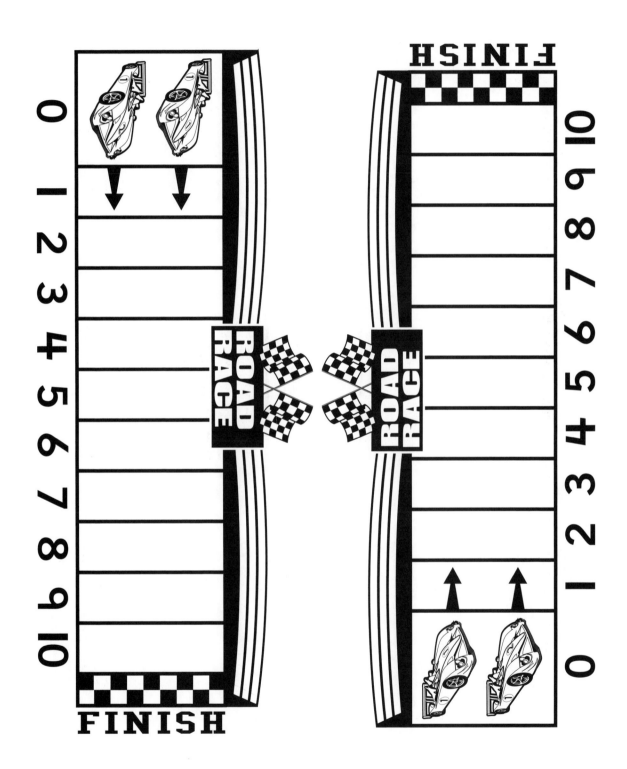

Template for Decimeter Rods

Template for Tabletop Rods

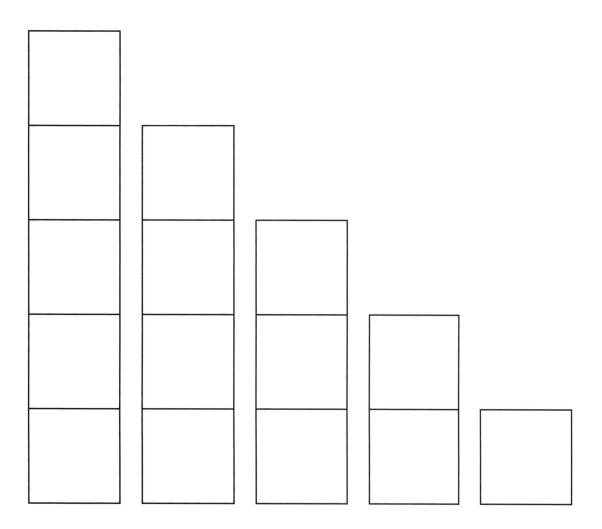

Sandpaper Numerals

0 1 2

3 4 5

6 7 8 9

Numeral Relay

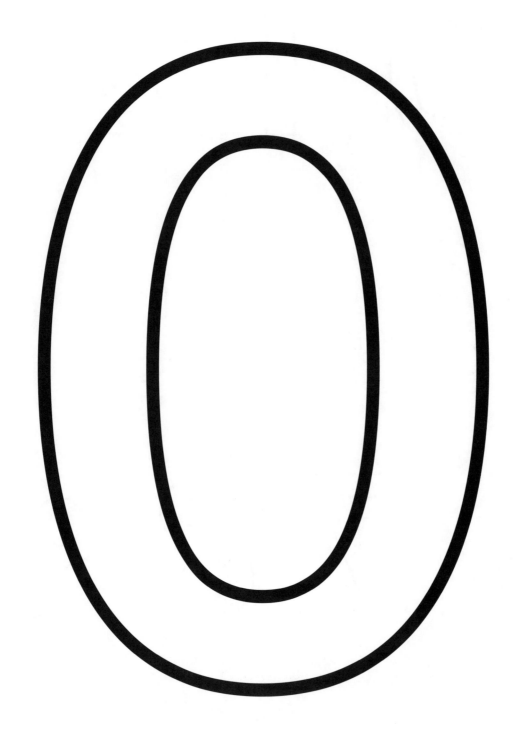

Numeral Relay

Numeral Relay

Numeral Relay

Numeral Relay

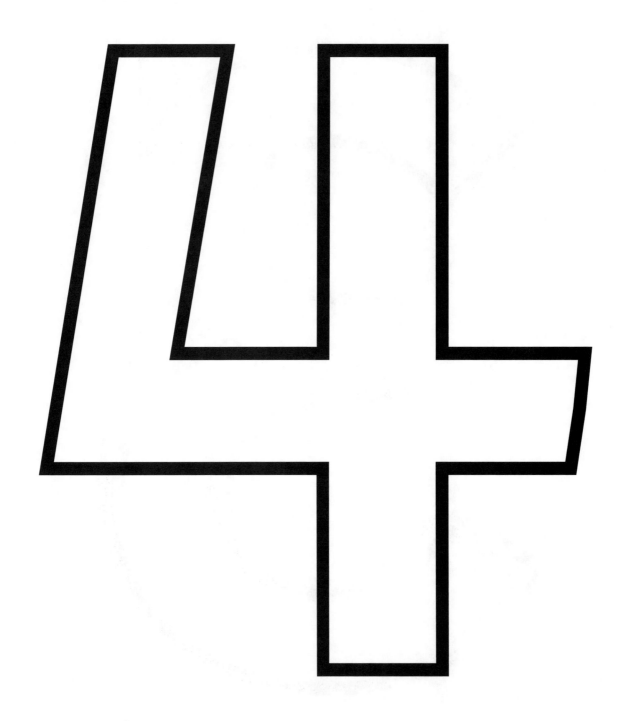

Numeral Relay

Numeral Relay

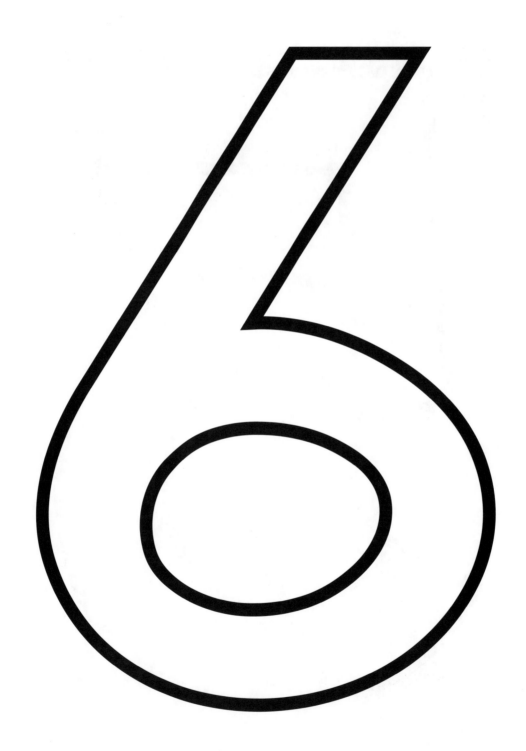

Numeral Relay

Numeral Relay

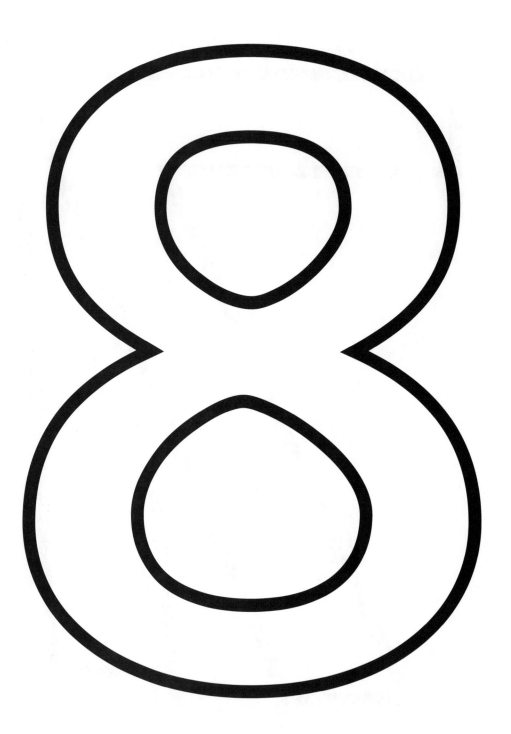

Numeral Relay

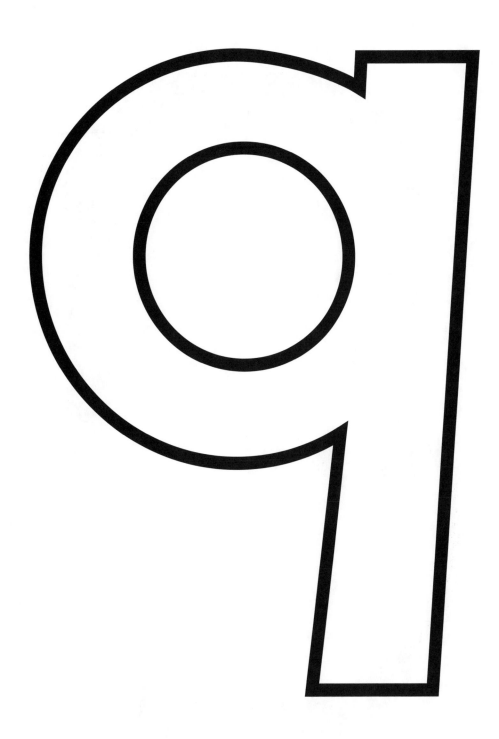

Path Cards

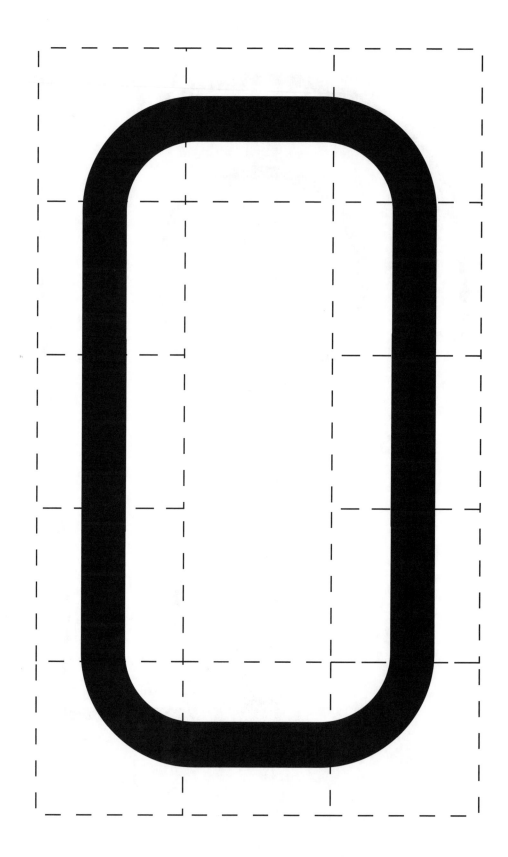

Path Cards

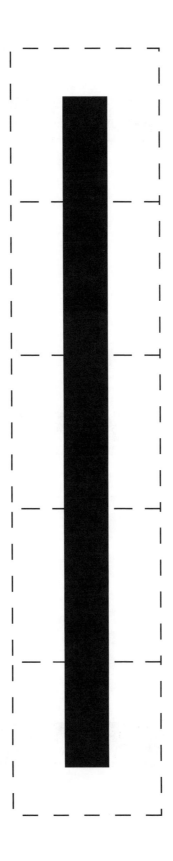

Path Cards

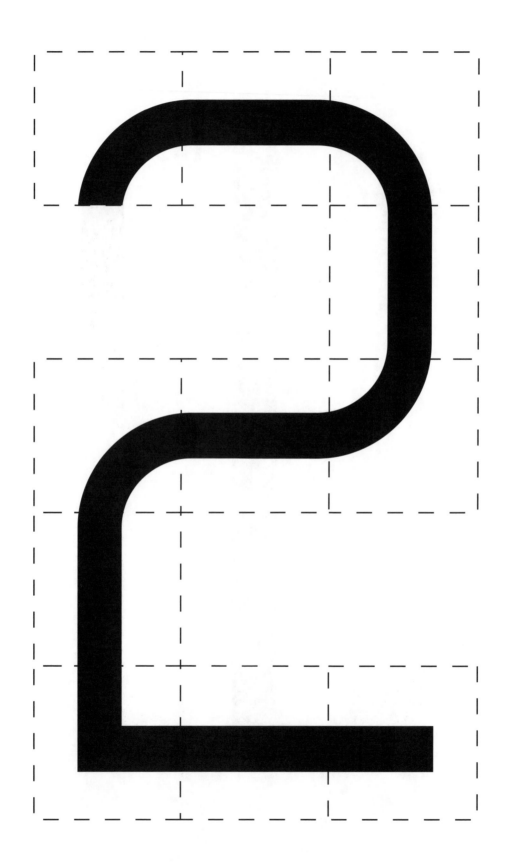

Path Cards

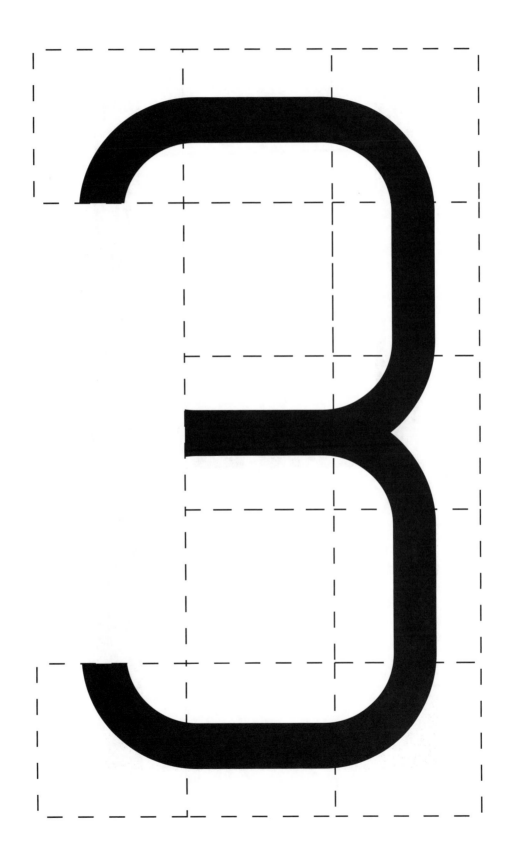

Path Cards

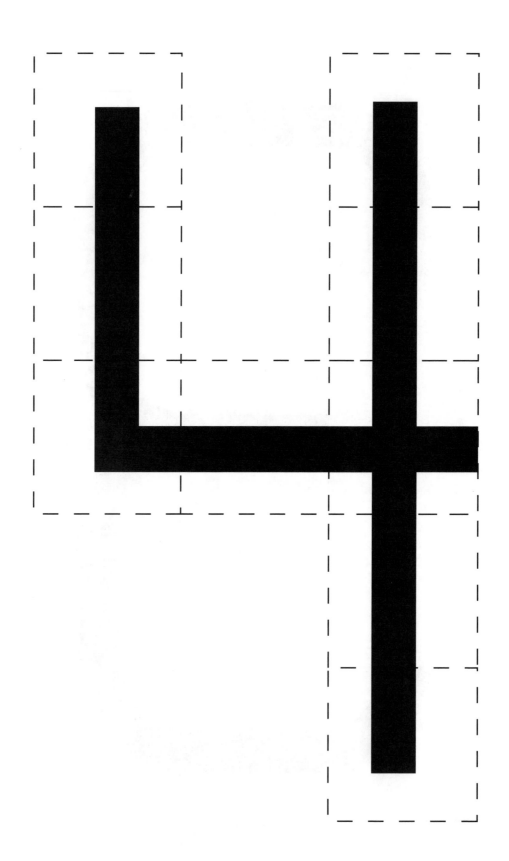

Path Cards

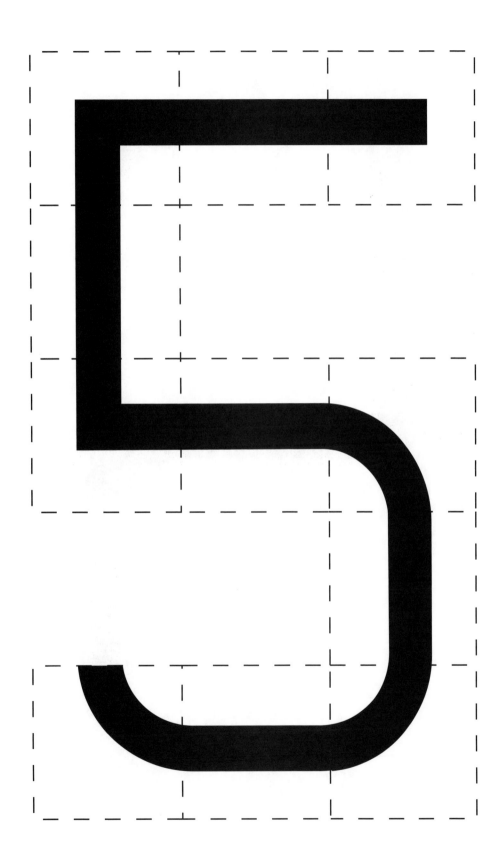

Path Cards

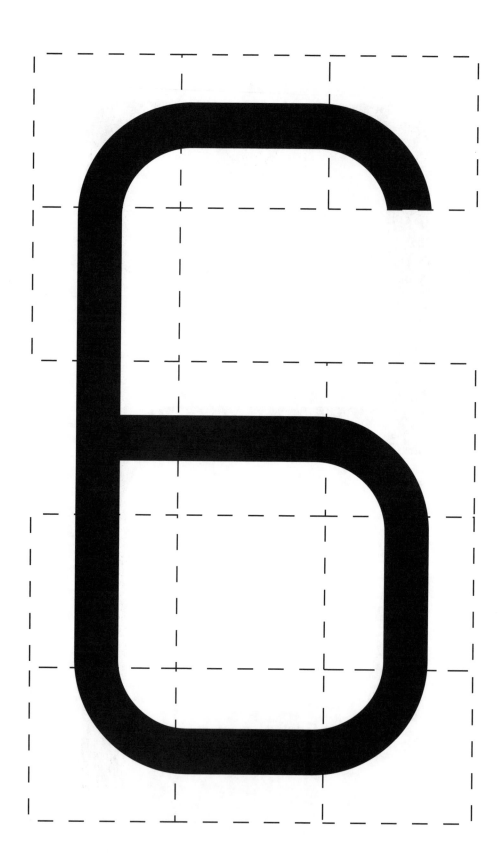

Path Cards

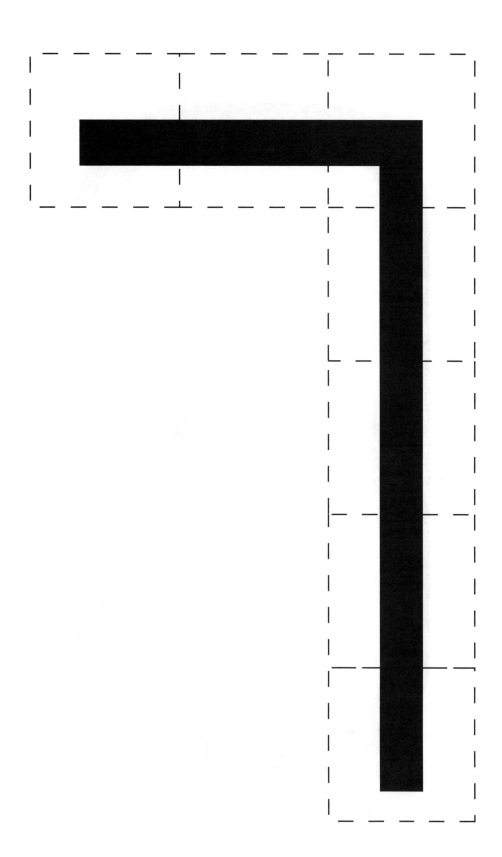

Path Cards

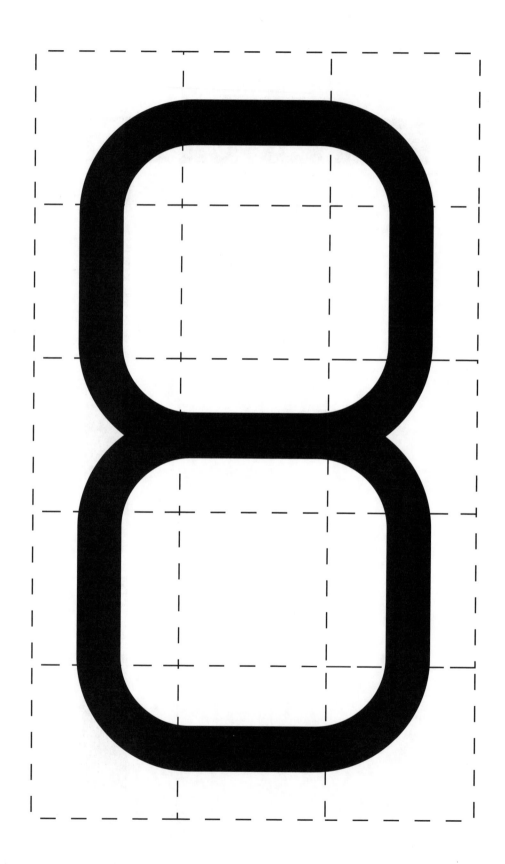

Path Cards

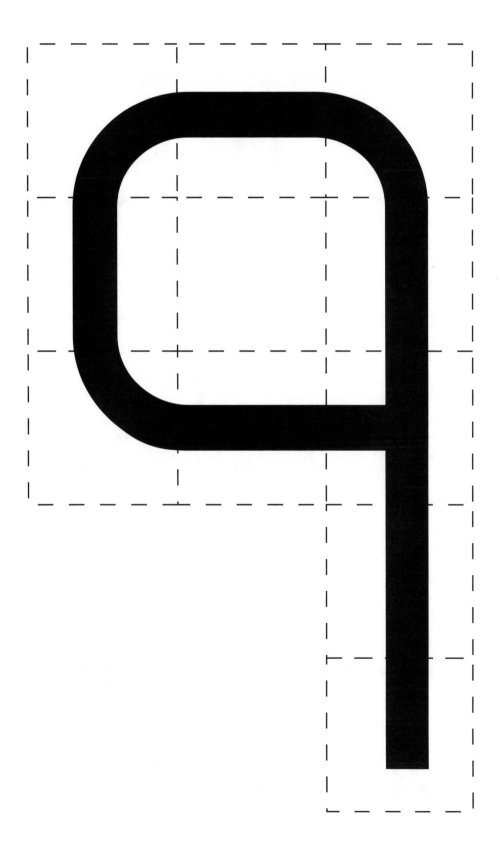

Bingo Cards for Number-Numeral Bingo

B	I	N	G	O

Parts-of Cards

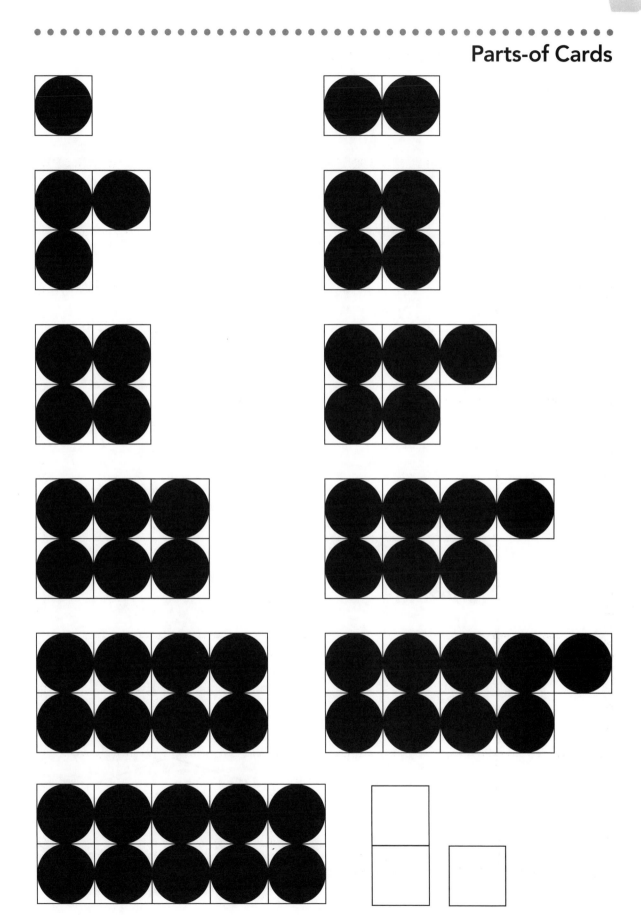

Pattern Blocks

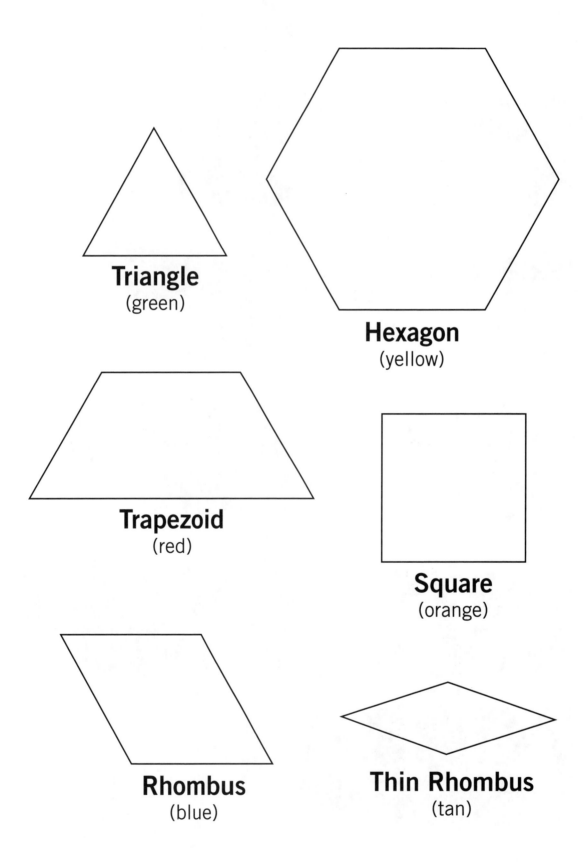

Triangle
(green)

Hexagon
(yellow)

Trapezoid
(red)

Square
(orange)

Rhombus
(blue)

Thin Rhombus
(tan)

Worm Hunt Game Pieces

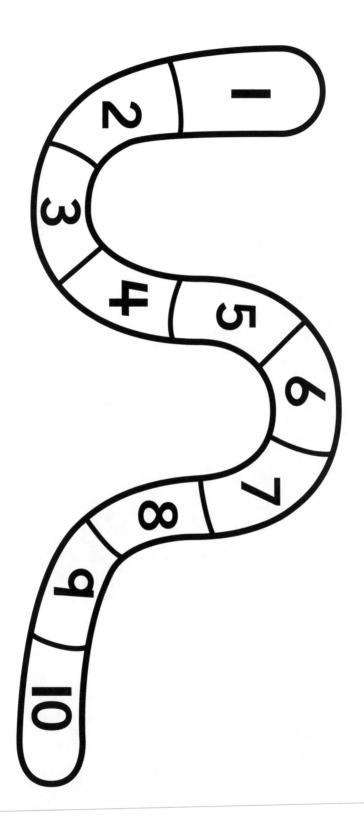

More/Less Spinner

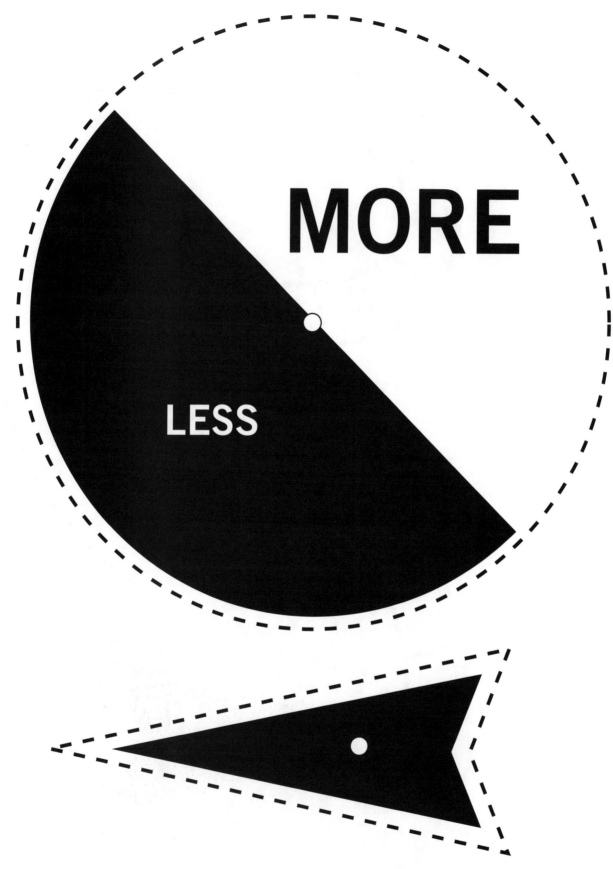

1 to 6 Spinner Showing Numerals

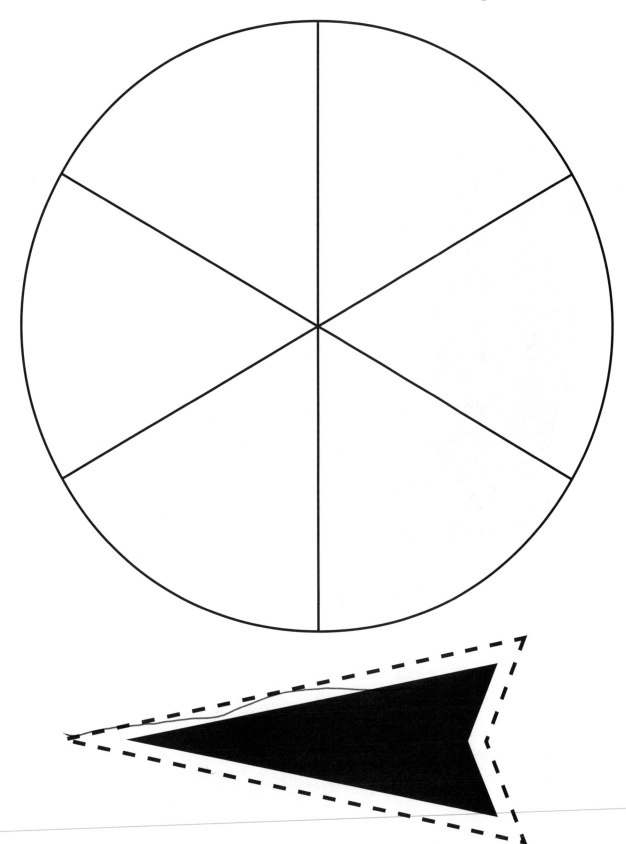

Die

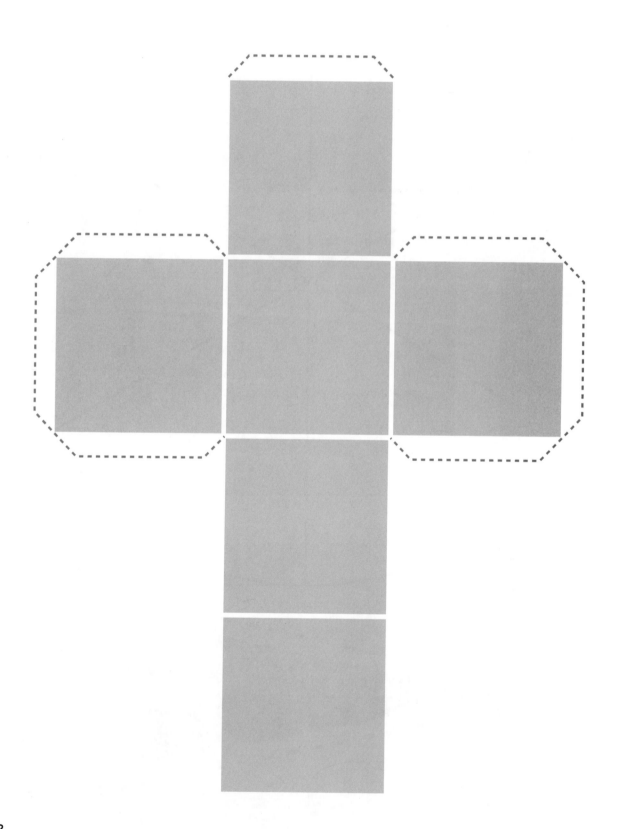

Dreidel Top Template

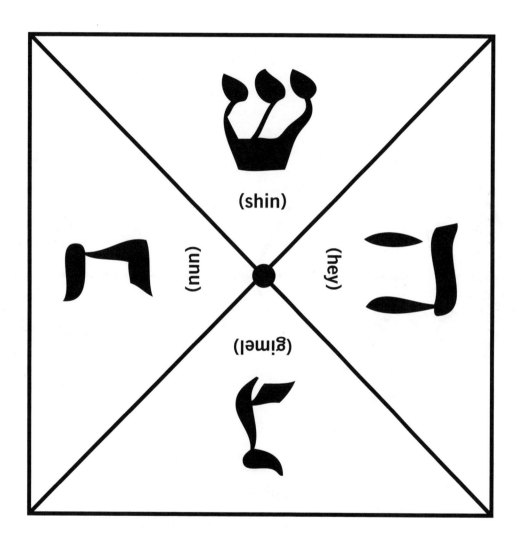

Toma-Todo Top Template

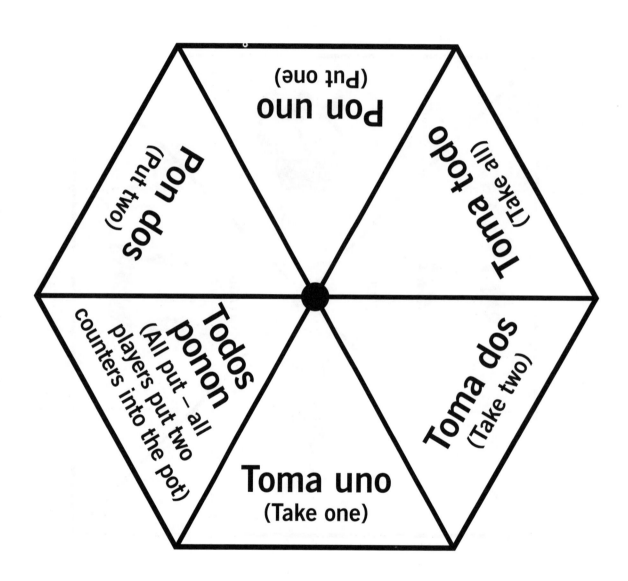

Patolli Board

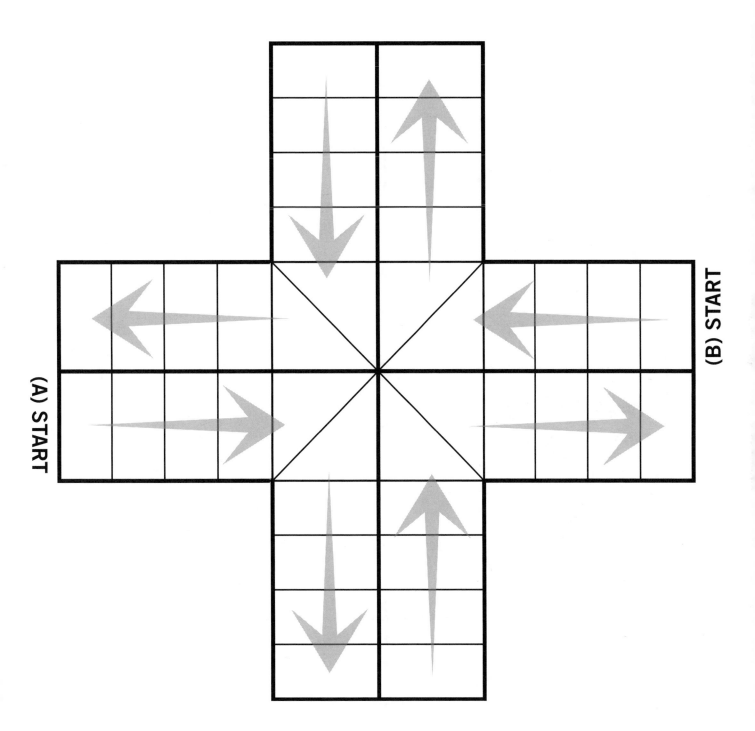

Kawasusuts Board

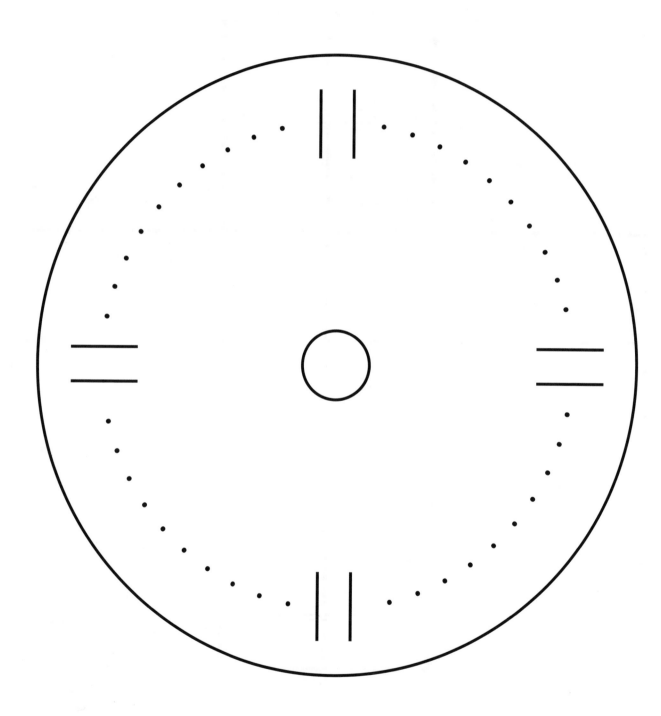

Feed the Squirrel